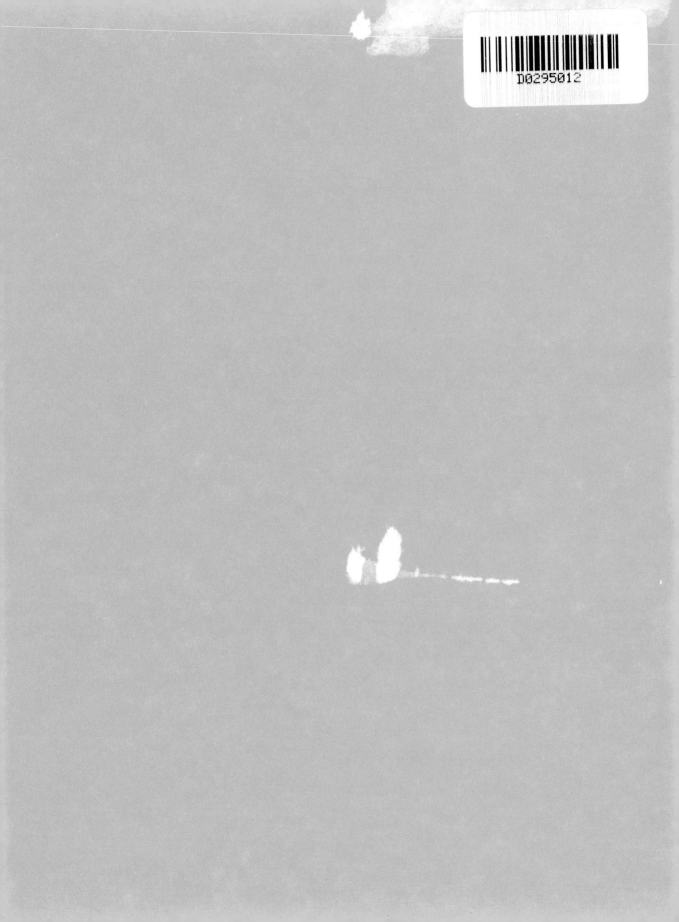

Anton Edelmann's
Perfect
Pastries, Puddings & Desserts

HarperCollins*Publishers*

Anton Edelmann's Perfect

Pastries, Puddings & Desserts

A stunning collection of delicious recipes to suit every occasion

Notes on the recipes

Always use medium eggs unless otherwise stated.
Always use unwaxed oranges and lemons whenever citrus rind is needed.
All spoon measurements are level unless otherwise stated.
Metric and imperial measurements have been calculated separately.
Always follow one set of measurements within a recipe.

First published in 1996 by HarperCollins*Publishers* London

Text © Anton Edelmann 1996
Illustrations & Photographs © HarperCollins*Publishers* 1996

A CIP catalogue record for this book is available from the British Library.

ISBN 0 00 414011 7

Packaged for HarperCollins*Publishers* by Rosemary Wilkinson, 4 Lonsdale Square, London N1 1EN.

EDITOR: Janet Illsley
DESIGNER: Sara Kidd
ILLUSTRATOR: Madeleine David
FOOD PHOTOGRAPHER: Steve Baxter
HOME ECONOMIST: Jane Stevenson

For HarperCollins*Publishers*:
COMMISSIONING EDITOR: Barbara Dixon
PRODUCTION MANAGER: Bridget Scanlon

Colour reproductions by Saxon Photolitho, Norwich, England.
Printed and bound by Rotolitho Lombarda S.p.A., Milan, Italy

CONTENTS

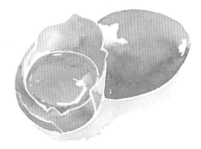

INTRODUCTION

"The delicious lunch was rounded off with an elegant dessert consisting of a white milk chocolate sorbet between layers of wafer-thin chocolate, swimming in a pool of orange sauce and decorated with summer berries."

She went on to describe the subtle flavours in great detail, sounding excited and animated, as if she was eating it all over again! "I will never eat another chocolate bar!" she added. Her eighteen-year-old companion in the underground carriage ... between Holborn and Covent Garden ... looked suitably impressed.

Why do we all love these sweet cakes, gâteaux, ice creams, sorbets and desserts?

The art of pastry-making goes back a very long time. The first step in its evolution must have been the baking of bread, which we now know was practised long ago by the ancient Egyptians. Since then, the development of this culinary art has gathered momentum and most civilizations and nations have left their mark.

The classic pâtisserie of yesteryear is, of course, still with us and forms the basis of what we do today. In recent years, we have cut back considerably on the quantities of eggs, butter, cream and sugar – to make pastries lighter, fluffier and healthier. Decorations are now far less elaborate ... yet simplicity of presentation seems to enhance rather than lessen the appeal of the food.

Why in this modern age of supermarket shopping, where everything is easily available, should we make the effort to produce desserts ourselves?

For me pastry work is one of the most satisfying, creative and pleasing of culinary crafts. I see it as one of the threads that binds us to the past and to each other. It reminds me of the heavenly aroma of a freshly baked Christmas stollen; the distinctive scents of cloves, hot raisins and roasted almonds; the rich, sweet smell of hot chocolate sponge cooling on a rack; the strong flavours of summer berries marinating in cassis and dry white wine; the cool, delicate flavours of sorbets; scrumptious ice creams; the contrast of bitter chocolate and sweet fresh orange. These wonderful fragrances create and heighten our anticipation.

To use this book to its full advantage, you do not need to be an experienced pastry chef, but you should remember that even the simplest and shortest recipe benefits from careful planning. To make sure you can repeat a favourite dish successfully, you need to be accurate and precise in the way you measure and prepare the ingredients.

Mastering the art of pastry preparation is all about continuous observation and endless curiosity. Perfection comes with practice. Do not attempt to do the impossible and always choose recipes you can cook with confidence. Leave nothing to chance!

The dessert or cake you serve should be an expression of your own personality and style. Your philosophy should be to aim for true flavours, lightness of texture and definition of taste ... and the results should be clear, simple and unfussy.

Finally, not only is the preparation of cakes, pastries and desserts in itself satisfying, there is immense pleasure to be gained from sitting down in the company of your friends and family to eat and enjoy your labour of love!

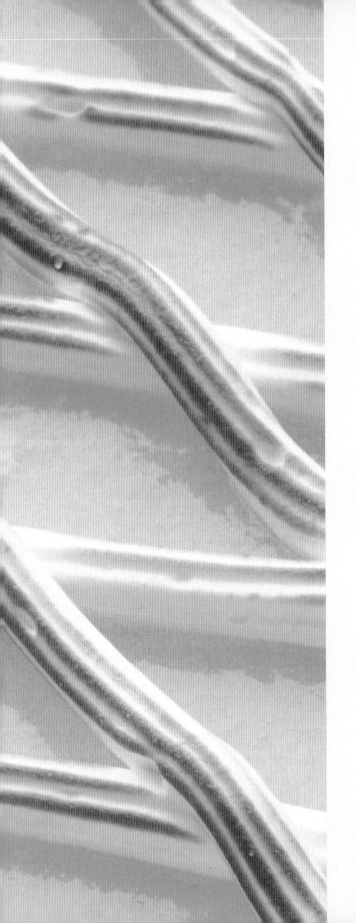

SPRING

Passion Fruit and Quark Soufflé

Mango and Passion Fruit Crumble

Pancakes with Plum Compote

Honey Fruit Salad

Lemon Tartlets

Exotic Fruit Mille Feuille

Simple Chocolate Tart

Waffles

Waffles with Pineapple

Waffles with Mango Sauce

Chocolate Waffles

Rhubarb, Rhubarb, Rhubarb

Grapefruit Meringue Gâteau

Apple Bakewell Tart

Traditional Provençal Dried Fig Cake

Dobos Torte

Liquorice Ice Cream

Cashew Nut Ice Cream

Marsala Almond Cake

Carrot Cake

Japanese Fruit Cake

Simnel Cake

Hot Cross Buns

Raisin and Honey Scones

PASSION FRUIT AND QUARK SOUFFLÉ

SERVES 6

When you prepare the soufflé dishes for this impressive dessert, be sure to butter and sugar the insides and rims well, to prevent the soufflés from sticking as they rise during baking.

10 passion fruit
2 egg yolks (size 2)
370 g (13 oz) quark cheese
finely grated zest of 1 lemon

3 tbsp light rum
5 tsp cornflour
8 tbsp icing sugar
3 egg whites (size 2)

1 Preheat the oven to 220°C/425°F/Gas Mark 7. Cut the passion fruit in half and scoop out the pulp and seeds into a bowl, using a teaspoon.
2 Generously butter 6 individual soufflé dishes, about 8 cm (3¼ inches) in diameter and 3.5 cm (1¼ inches) deep, then dust out with sugar. (This prevents the soufflé mixture from sticking as it is baking.) Chill in the refrigerator while preparing the mixture.
3 Put the egg yolks, quark, grated lemon zest, rum, half of the passion fruit pulp, 2½ tsp cornflour and 4 tbsp icing sugar into a large bowl. Beat well until evenly blended.
4 In another large clean bowl, whisk the egg whites until stiff, then whisk in the remaining icing sugar to make a light meringue. Stir a spoonful into the quark mixture to loosen it,

then gently fold in the rest of the meringue using a large metal spoon.
5 Divide the mixture between the prepared soufflé dishes. Set them in a bain-marie (or roasting tin containing enough cold water to come halfway up the sides of the dishes). Bake in the oven for about 15 minutes or until well risen and golden.
6 Meanwhile, mix the rest of the cornflour with 2 tbsp passion fruit pulp. Heat the rest of the passion fruit in a saucepan, then stir in the cornflour mixture. Simmer, stirring, for about 1 minute until thickened.
7 Remove the soufflés from the bain-marie and loosen the sides with a small sharp knife. Turn each one out upside down onto the centre of a warmed serving plate. Spoon the passion fruit sauce around the soufflés and serve immediately.

MANGO AND PASSION FRUIT CRUMBLE

SERVES 4

2 passion fruit
3 mangoes, peeled, stoned and diced
60 g (2 oz) caster sugar
90 g (3 oz) walnuts, chopped

90 g (3 oz) soft brown sugar
120 g (6 oz) plain flour, sifted
60 g (2 oz) butter, melted
icing sugar for dusting

1 Preheat oven to 180°C/350°F/Gas Mark 4. Halve the passion fruit and scoop out the pulp into a saucepan. Add the diced mangoes and caster sugar. Cook gently over a low heat until the mango is softened. Transfer the fruit to a 600 ml (1 pint) ovenproof dish.

2 In a bowl, mix the chopped walnuts with the brown sugar and flour. Add the butter and stir to form a rough crumble.
3 Spoon the crumble over the fruit and bake in the oven for 25 minutes.
4 Dust with icing sugar to serve.

PANCAKES WITH PLUM COMPOTE

SERVES 4

8 Pancakes (see below)

PLUM COMPOTE

250 g (8½ oz) sugar

180 ml (6 fl oz) water

½ cinnamon stick

1 clove

strip of finely pared lemon zest

400 g (14 oz) plums, halved and stoned

TO SERVE

icing sugar for dusting

1 Put the sugar and water in a medium saucepan and heat gently until the sugar is dissolved, then add the cinnamon stick, clove and lemon zest and bring to the boil.

2 Add the plum halves to the syrup and cook gently until just tender. Remove with a slotted spoon and peel away the skins; in the meantime boil the syrup to reduce down until syrupy. Return the fruit to the syrup and set aside for 5-10 minutes.

3 To serve, place a spoonful of the plum compote on each pancake and fold one half over. Place two pancakes on each plate and dust with icing sugar to serve.

PANCAKES

120 g (4 oz) plain flour

pinch of salt

1 egg

300 ml (½ pint) milk

a little oil for frying

1 Sift the flour and salt into a bowl and make a well in the centre. Add the egg with about a quarter of the milk and mix to a thick smooth paste. Slowly whisk in the rest of the milk to form a smooth, thin pouring batter.

2 To cook the pancakes, very lightly oil an 18 cm (7 inch) heavy-based crêpe pan. Place over a medium high heat until very hot.

3 Using a ladle, pour in just enough batter to cover the base thinly, tilting the pan to spread the batter evenly. Cook for 30 seconds or until set on top and the underside is golden brown. Toss or flip over using a palette knife and cook for a further 30 seconds until the underside is golden. Turn out onto a plate to serve.

NOTE: To keep pancakes warm for a short time, stack them in a pile on a warmed plate interleaved with greaseproof paper to keep them moist.

Mango and Passion Fruit Crumble (page 11); Pancakes with Plum Compote

HONEY FRUIT SALAD

SERVES 4

1 Granny Smith apple, peeled, quartered and cored
1 orange, peeled and segmented
1 banana, peeled
2 kiwi fruit, peeled
1 mango, peeled and stoned
½ baby pineapple, peeled and cored
8 strawberries, hulled

FOR THE SYRUP
125 ml (4 fl oz) water
4 tbsp honey
8 strips of lemon zest
1 tbsp lemon juice
3 tbsp orange juice

1 First make the syrup. Put the water, honey and lemon zest into a saucepan and slowly bring to the boil over a low heat. Simmer, stirring occasionally, for 2 minutes. Remove from the heat and allow to cool.

2 Strain the syrup through a fine sieve into a large bowl. Add the lemon and orange juices.
3 Cut the fruit into slices, immediately adding it to the syrup, to ensure that it doesn't discolour. Chill for 1 hour before serving.

LEMON TARTLETS

MAKES 16

200 g (7 oz) Sweet Pastry (see below)

FOR THE FILLING

100 g (3½ oz) caster sugar

3 eggs

finely grated zest of 2 lemons

2 tbsp lemon juice

75 g (2½ oz) unsalted butter, cut into cubes

1 Roll out the pastry on a lightly floured surface and use to line 16 tartlet tins, 5 cm (2 inches) in diameter and 2 cm (¾ inch) deep. Line with greaseproof paper and fill with baking beans. Chill in the refrigerator for 20 minutes. Meanwhile, preheat the oven to 200°C/400°F/Gas Mark 6.
2 Bake the pastry cases for 10 minutes, then remove the paper and beans and bake for a further 5 minutes, until golden brown.
3 For the lemon filling, place the sugar, eggs, lemon zest and juice in a saucepan and cook over a very gentle heat, whisking constantly, until the mixture thickens – do not allow to boil or it will curdle. Remove from the heat and whisk in the butter, a few pieces at a time.
4 Allow the filling to cool, then pipe or spoon into the tartlet cases.

SWEET PASTRY

You will need about one third of this pastry quantity to line a 20 cm (8 inch) flan tin, or 4 individual flan tins, or 16 tartlet tins. Divide the dough into 3 portions. Wrap and freeze the portions you don't need to use immediately, or keep in the refrigerator for up to 3 days.

225 g (8 oz) unsalted butter

100 g (3½ oz) caster sugar

1 egg, beaten

350 g (12 oz) plain flour, sifted

pinch of salt

1 Cream the butter and sugar together in a bowl until very pale, then beat in the egg a little at a time. Gradually add the flour with the salt and mix to a smooth dough.
2 Cover and leave to rest in a cool place, ideally for 12-24 hours.

EXOTIC FRUIT MILLE FEUILLE

MAKES 4

As an alternative to exotic fruits, use a selection of summer berries, such as strawberries, raspberries, blueberries and blackberries.

12 circles of filo pastry, 10 cm (4 inches) in diameter
100 ml (3½ fl oz) double cream
2 tbsp icing sugar
100 ml (3½ fl oz) Greek yoghurt
200 g (7 oz) prepared mixed exotic fruits, such as mango, pawpaw, kiwi, pineapple (peeled, seeded and cut into cubes)

TO DECORATE
icing sugar for dusting
mint sprigs
extra exotic fruit (optional)
TO SERVE
Strawberry or Raspberry Coulis (see below)

1 Preheat oven to 200°C/400°F/Gas Mark 6. Place the filo circles individually on greased baking sheets. Brush lightly with water and bake for 10-15 minutes until golden and lightly puffed up. Leave to cool.
2 In a bowl, whip the double cream with the icing sugar until it forms soft peaks, then stir in the yoghurt.
3 Carefully fold the exotic fruit into the cream mixture.

4 Place a filo pastry disc on each serving plate and spoon a little of the fruit mixture on top. Cover with another filo disc, add more fruit and top with a third filo disc.
5 Repeat to make 3 more desserts in the same way.
6 Dust the tops of the mille feuille with icing sugar. Decorate with mint sprigs and extra fruit, if wished. Pour a little coulis around each dessert and serve at once.

STRAWBERRY OR RASPBERRY COULIS

200 g (7 oz) strawberries, halved, or raspberries

30-45 g (1-1½ oz) icing sugar
1 tsp lemon juice

Place the strawberries or raspberries, icing sugar and lemon juice in a blender or food processor and work to a purée, then pass through a fine sieve into a bowl to remove the seeds.

SIMPLE CHOCOLATE TART

SERVES 6

200 g (7 oz) Sweet Pastry (see page 15)
150 g (5 oz) plain dark chocolate
2 egg yolks
1 egg

30 g (1 oz) caster sugar
100 g (3½ oz) unsalted butter, softened
TO FINISH
icing sugar for dusting

1 Roll out the sweet pastry on a lightly floured surface to a 3 mm (⅛ inch) thickness and use to line a 15 cm (6 inch) loose-bottomed flan tin (or flan ring placed on a baking sheet). Line the pastry case with greaseproof paper and weight it down with baking beans. Leave to rest in the refrigerator for 20 minutes. Meanwhile, preheat the oven to 190°C/375°F/Gas Mark 5.
2 Bake the pastry case blind for 15 minutes, then remove the paper and baking beans and bake for a further 5-10 minutes to cook the base. Allow to cool. Reduce the oven setting to

180°C/350°F/Gas Mark 4.
3 Melt the chocolate in a heatproof bowl over a pan of simmering water and stir until smooth; cool slightly.
4 Meanwhile, beat the egg yolks, whole egg and sugar together in a bowl until creamy. Slowly pour on the melted chocolate, stirring all the time. Finally, beat in the softened butter.
5 Pour the chocolate filling into the pastry case and bake in the oven for 10-12 minutes, until just firm.
6 Allow to cool. Serve dusted with icing sugar.

Raisin and Honey Scones (page 37); Waffles with Pineapple

WAFFLES

SERVES 4

2 eggs, separated
2 tbsp vegetable oil
175 ml (6 fl oz) milk
100 g (3½ oz) plain flour

1 tsp baking powder
pinch of salt
45 g (1½ oz) caster sugar
icing sugar for dusting

1 Whisk the egg yolks together with the oil and milk.
2 Sift the flour, baking powder and salt together into a bowl and stir in the sugar. Mix in the liquid to give a smooth batter.
3 In a separate bowl, whisk the egg whites until they form soft peaks, then fold into the batter.
4 Lightly oil a large waffle iron and preheat on the hob for 1-2 minutes.
5 Spoon about a quarter of the mixture on to the waffle iron and close it. Cook over a medium heat for about 2 minutes on each side until crisp and golden brown. Remove and keep warm. Make 3 or 4 more waffles in the same way.
6 Serve dusted with icing sugar.

WAFFLES WITH PINEAPPLE

SERVES 4

4 Waffles (see above)
1 baby pineapple
10 cloves

10 black peppercorns
500 g (1 lb 2 oz) sugar
500 ml (16 fl oz) water

1 To prepare the pineapple, top and tail, then peel away the skin. Slice crosswise into 1 cm (½ inch) thick rounds, then remove the core with a small cutter.
2 Stud each pineapple slice with 2 cloves and grind the peppercorns on to the slices.
3 Dissolve the sugar in the water in a saucepan over a low heat, then bring to the boil. Add the pineapple rings to the sugar syrup and poach for 2-3 minutes over a low heat.
4 Remove the pineapple rings from the sugar syrup with a slotted spoon; boil the syrup to reduce.
5 Place the pineapple on warmed serving plates with the hot waffles. Spoon a little of the syrup over the pineapple. Serve at once.

WAFFLES WITH MANGO SAUCE

SERVES 4

4 Waffles (see page 19)
FOR THE MANGO SAUCE
100 ml (3½ fl oz) water

1 tsp sugar
1 mango, peeled, stoned and diced
2 tbsp yoghurt

1 To make the mango sauce, bring the water to the boil in a saucepan and add the sugar, stirring to dissolve.
2 Put the mango in a blender or food processor with the sugar syrup and process until smooth.
3 Allow to cool, then add the yoghurt. Pass the sauce through a fine sieve into a bowl.
4 Serve the hot waffles with the mango sauce.

CHOCOLATE WAFFLES

SERVES 6

110 g (3¾ oz) self-raising flour
1 tbsp cocoa powder
pinch of salt
2 tsp sugar
200 ml (7 fl oz) milk
3 egg yolks

1 tbsp olive oil
1½ egg whites
FOR THE VANILLA MASCARPONE
150 g (5 oz) mascarpone cheese
1 vanilla pod, split

1 First prepare the vanilla marscapone. Put the mascarpone into a bowl, stir in the vanilla seeds, cover and place in the refrigerator until required.
2 To make the waffles, sift the flour, cocoa powder and salt together into a bowl and stir in the sugar. Stir in half of the milk.
3 Add the rest of the milk, the egg yolks and olive oil to give a smooth, creamy batter.
4 Whisk the egg whites in a separate bowl until they form soft peaks, then fold into the batter.
5 Lightly oil a large waffle iron and preheat on the hob for 1-2 minutes.
6 Spoon about a quarter of the mixture onto the waffle iron, close it and cook over a medium heat for 2 minutes on each side, until crisp. Take out and keep warm. Make 3 or 4 more waffles in the same way.
7 Serve dusted with icing sugar, accompanied by the vanilla-flavoured mascarpone.

RHUBARB, RHUBARB, RHUBARB

SERVES 4

800 g (1¾ lb) rhubarb
250 g (8½ oz) caster sugar
700 ml (scant 1¼ pints) water
150 g (5 oz) soft brown sugar

finely grated zest of 1 lemon
1 gelatine leaf
1 tbsp Ribena concentrate

1 Preheat the oven to 50°C/120°F/Gas Mark ⅛. Peel the rhubarb and cut 2 sticks into 7 cm (2¾ inch) lengths. Put 100 g (3½ oz) of the caster sugar in a saucepan with 100 ml (3½ fl oz) water. Dissolve over a low heat, then bring to the boil and simmer for 1 minute. Remove from the heat and allow to cool.

2 Using a swivel vegetable peeler, cut the 7 cm (2¾ inch) rhubarb lengths into fine perfect strips. Dip these into the syrup, one at a time, shake well and place on a wire rack. When you have 20 strips, place in the warm oven for 30 minutes to dry out, then allow to cool. Keep the crystallized rhubarb in an airtight container until ready to use.

3 To make the sorbet, cut 500 g (1 lb 2 oz) of the rhubarb into small pieces. Put the brown sugar in a saucepan with 350 ml (12 fl oz) water and half of the lemon zest. Dissolve over a low heat, then bring the syrup to the boil. Add the rhubarb, cover and simmer until tender. Allow to cool, then purée in a food processor and pass through a fine sieve into a measuring jug. If necessary make up to 500 ml (16 fl oz) purée with water.

4 Freeze the rhubarb purée in an ice-cream machine according to the manufacturer's instructions. Alternatively pour into a freezer-proof container and freeze until almost set. Transfer to a food processor and whizz to break down the ice crystals. Return to the container and freeze. Repeat this process twice to ensure a fine-textured sorbet, then freeze until firm.

5 For the rhubarb compote, cut the remaining rhubarb into 3 cm (1¼ inch) sticks. Soak the gelatine leaf in cold water to cover for about 10 minutes to soften. Meanwhile put the remaining caster sugar in a shallow pan with 250 ml (8 fl oz) water and the Ribena. Dissolve over a low heat, then bring to the boil. Add the rhubarb and remaining lemon zest, and simmer until the rhubarb is tender, yet still retaining its shape. Remove the rhubarb with a slotted spoon and set aside to cool.

6 Squeeze the excess water from the gelatine leaf, then add it to the cooking liquor, stirring until melted. Allow to cool; do not refrigerate.

7 To serve, divide the rhubarb between 4 soup plates and pour on sufficient liquor to just cover. Add 2 balls of sorbet to each serving and arrange a few crystallized rhubarb strips on top of the sorbet. Serve at once.

GRAPEFRUIT MERINGUE GÂTEAU

SERVES 8

FOR THE BISCUIT BASE

2 egg whites

100 g (3½ oz) caster sugar

40 g (1¼ oz) ground almonds

½ tsp plain flour

FOR THE FILLING AND TOPPING

5 gelatine leaves

180 ml (6 fl oz) grapefruit juice

finely grated zest of 2 grapefruit

200 g (7 oz) caster sugar

450 ml (¾ pint) whipping cream

2 egg whites

TO GLAZE

4 tbsp apricot jam

2 tbsp water

1 To make the biscuit base, preheat the oven to 150°C/300°F/Gas Mark 2. Draw a 20 cm (8 inch) circle on a sheet of non-stick baking parchment and invert the paper. Whisk the egg whites in a bowl until they form firm peaks. Gradually whisk in half of the sugar, then lightly fold in the rest, using a metal spoon. Fold in the ground almonds and flour.

2 Using a piping bag fitted with a 1 cm (½ inch) nozzle, pipe the mixture in a continuous spiral onto the baking parchment to cover the circle. Bake for 30 minutes to make a firm biscuit. Allow to cool, then place in a 20 cm (8 inch) round spring-release cake tin.

3 For the grapefruit mousse, soak the gelatine leaves in cold water to cover for about 10 minutes until softened.

4 Meanwhile put the grapefruit juice and zest in a heavy-based pan with 120 g (4 oz) of the sugar and dissolve over a low heat. Bring to the boil, then remove from the heat.

5 Squeeze out the water from the gelatine leaves, add to the warm grapefruit syrup and stir until melted. Pass through a sieve into a bowl. Set over a large bowl of iced water to cool, stirring occasionally until it starts to thicken.

6 In the meantime, whip the cream in another bowl until soft peaks form. Fold into the grapefruit mixture.

7 Quickly pour the grapefruit mousse onto the biscuit base and level the surface to give a smooth finish. Chill in the refrigerator for at least 4 hours until set.

8 Whisk the egg whites in a bowl until they form stiff peaks, then gradually whisk in the rest of the sugar, a spoonful at a time, to make a firm glossy meringue.

9 Mix the apricot jam and water together in a small pan and bring to the boil. Cool slightly, then brush thinly over the top of the mousse.

10 Carefully unmould the gâteau. Using a piping bag fitted with a small fluted nozzle, pipe a meringue lattice over the top, and a border. Place under a preheated hot grill for 30 seconds to 1 minute, until the meringue is tinged golden brown, or quickly scorch using a blow torch.

Grapefruit Meringue Gâteau

APPLE BAKEWELL TART

SERVES 8

250 g (8½ oz) Sweet Pastry (see page 15)
200 g (7 oz) butter
200 g (7 oz) caster sugar
3 eggs
200 g (7 oz) ground almonds
20 g (¾ oz) plain flour
1 tbsp rum

60 g (2 oz) apple jam
1 Cox's apple
TO FINISH
150 g (5 oz) Fondant (see below)
2 tbsp water
40 g (1¼ oz) plain dark chocolate

1 Roll out the pastry on a lightly floured surface to a 5 mm (¼ inch) thickness and use to line a deep 23 cm (9 inch) loose-bottomed flan ring (or flan ring placed on a baking sheet). Leave to rest in the refrigerator for 20 minutes. Preheat the oven to 200°C/400°F/Gas Mark 6.
2 Meanwhile, cream the butter and sugar together in a bowl until light and fluffy. Beat in the eggs, one at a time, then fold in the ground almonds, flour and rum.
3 Spread the apple jam over the base of the pastry case. Peel, core and slice the apple, then scatter over the jam in the pastry case. Spoon the almond mixture on top and smooth the surface.
4 Bake in the oven for 10-15 minutes. Reduce

the oven temperature to 180°C/350°F/Gas Mark 4 and bake for a further 25-30 minutes until golden. Allow to cool.
5 For the topping, place the fondant and water in a pan and warm very gently over a low heat, stirring constantly, until smooth. Remove from the heat. Meanwhile melt the chocolate in a bowl over a pan of hot water; stir until smooth.
6 Spread the warm fondant evenly over the tart with a palette knife. Using a greaseproof paper piping bag, quickly pipe fine parallel lines of melted chocolate across the tart. Draw a cocktail stick alternately back and forth across the chocolate lines to create a feathered pattern. Leave until set.

FONDANT

pinch of cream of tartar
175 ml (6 fl oz) water

1 kg (2¼ lb) caster sugar
60 ml (2 fl oz) liquid glucose

1 Mix the cream of tartar with a little of the water to a paste.
2 Put the sugar and remaining water in a

heavy-based saucepan and dissolve over a low heat. Increase the heat and bring the sugar syrup to the boil. Add the liquid glucose and

Summer Fruit Trifle

MARINATED SUMMER FRUIT

SERVES 4

juice of 3 limes
150 ml (¼ pint) dry white wine
4 tbsp crème de cassis
60 g (2 oz) icing sugar, sifted
2 tsp chopped mint

350 g (12 oz) mixed summer berries, such as raspberries, strawberries, black-berries, blueberries and loganberries

TO SERVE
Raspberry Sorbet (see page 67)
Almond Biscotti (see below)

1 Mix the lime juice, white wine and crème de cassis together in a bowl. Add the icing sugar and whisk well to mix. Stir in the chopped mint. Cover and chill in the refrigerator for at least 1 hour.
2 Divide the berries between 4 small soup plates. Pass the lime mixture through a fine sieve into a bowl, then spoon over the berries.
3 Shape the sorbet into quenelles or ovals, using a tablespoon dipped in hot water.
4 Position the sorbet on top of the berries and serve at once, with almond biscotti if wished.

ALMOND BISCOTTI

1 star anise
220 g (7¾ oz) plain flour
130 g (4¼ oz) icing sugar
pinch of salt

3 eggs, lightly beaten
finely grated zest of 1 orange
100 g (3½ oz) blanched almonds, toasted

1 Finely grind the star anise, using a mortar and pestle.
2 Sift the flour, icing sugar and salt into a bowl and make a well in the centre.
3 Add the eggs, ground star anise and grated orange zest to the well. Mix thoroughly to a sticky dough. Knead in the toasted almonds.
4 Shape the dough into a log, about 4 cm (1½ inches) in diameter. Wrap in non-stick baking parchment and chill in the freezer for 1 hour until firm.
5 Preheat oven to 180°C/350°F/Gas Mark 4. Place the log, still in the baking parchment, on a baking sheet. Bake for 50-55 minutes or until golden brown.
6 Allow to cool, then cut into 20-24 very thin slices, about 2 mm (½ inch) thick. Carefully transfer to a wire rack and leave to dry.

RASPBERRY CRÈME BRÛLÉE

SERVES 4

100 g (3½ oz) raspberries

6 tbsp eau de vie de framboises

4 egg yolks

90 g (3 oz) caster sugar

250 ml (8 fl oz) double cream

1 Put the raspberries in a bowl, sprinkle with the liqueur and leave to stand for about 30 minutes.

2 Preheat oven to 150°C/300°F/Gas Mark 2. Divide the raspberries and liqueur between 4 ramekins.

3 Whisk the egg yolks and 50 g (1¾ oz) of the sugar together in a bowl until pale, then stir in the cream. Pass the mixture through a fine sieve into a jug, then pour into the ramekins.

4 Stand the ramekins in a bain-marie (or roasting tin containing enough hot water to come halfway up the sides of the dishes). Cook in the oven for 30 minutes or until set.

5 Remove from the oven and allow to cool until lukewarm.

6 Sprinkle the surface of each crème generously with the remaining caster sugar. Caramelize under a preheated high grill (or using a blow torch). Serve warm or cold.

QUARK WITH RASPBERRIES

SERVES 4

200 g (7 oz) quark cheese
4 egg whites
45 g (1½ oz) caster sugar
200 ml (7 fl oz) double cream
finely grated zest of 1 lemon

½ tbsp vanilla sugar
200 g (7 oz) raspberries
TO SERVE
mint sprigs to decorate
Strawberry Coulis (see page 16)

1 Wrap the quark in muslin, then squeeze it to remove excess liquid and place in a bowl.
2 Whisk the egg whites in a bowl until they form stiff peaks, then whisk in the sugar a little at a time until the mixture is thick and glossy.
3 In another bowl, whip the cream until it forms soft peaks, add the lemon zest and vanilla sugar, then fold into the quark.
4 Fold in the egg white mixture and stir in half of the raspberries.
5 Spoon the quark mixture onto individual large serving plates and arrange the remaining raspberries on top. Decorate with sprigs of mint and surround with the strawberry coulis.

SUMMER PUDDING

SERVES 4

175 g (6 oz) white bread, thinly sliced and crusts removed

150 g (5 oz) strawberries

150 g (5 oz) blueberries

50 g (1¾ oz) raspberries

50 g (1¾ oz) red currants

50 g (1¾ oz) caster sugar

Blackcurrant Sauce (see below)

TO SERVE

30-60g (1-2 oz) wild strawberries

30-60g (1-2 oz) blueberries

30-60g (1-2 oz) raspberries

redcurrant sprigs to decorate

icing sugar for dusting

1 Cut 4 rounds of bread to fit the bases of four 180 ml (6 fl oz) dariole moulds (or individual pudding basins); cut 4 rounds to fit the tops and set aside. Cut the rest of the bread into 1 cm (¾ inch) wide fingers.

2 Line the bases of the moulds with the smaller bread rounds, then line the sides with the strips of bread.

3 Put the strawberries, blueberries, raspberries and red currants in a saucepan with the sugar and cook gently for about 10 minutes until the fruit is tender and the syrup is slightly reduced.

4 Spoon the hot fruit and syrup into the bread-lined moulds to fill them. Allow the bread to soak up the syrup, then add extra fruit as necessary to fill each mould completely.

5 Top with the reserved rounds of bread. Cover and chill in the refrigerator overnight.

6 To serve, unmould the summer puddings on to individual plates. Spoon some blackcurrant sauce over each pudding and decorate with the strawberries, blueberries, raspberries and sprigs of redcurrants. Dust with icing sugar and serve with cream.

BLACKCURRANT SAUCE

250 g (8½ oz) blackcurrants

150 ml (¼ pint) sugar syrup (see page 86)

Put the blackcurrants and sugar syrup in a blender or food processor and work to a purée. Pass through a fine sieve into a bowl to ensure a smooth sauce.

Blueberry Cheesecake; Summer Pudding (page 51)

BLUEBERRY CHEESECAKE

SERVES 8

one 20 cm (8 inch) Shortbread round (see below)
500 g (1 lb 2 oz) Philadelphia cream cheese
110 g (3¾ oz) caster sugar
15 g (½ oz) cornflour

finely grated zest of 1 orange
2 eggs
300 ml (½ pint) double cream
90 g (3 oz) blueberries
icing sugar for dusting

1 Grease and line a 20 cm (8 inch) springform cake tin. Preheat oven to 150°C/300°F/Gas Mark 2.
2 Beat the cream cheese, sugar, cornflour and orange zest together in a bowl until smooth. Gradually beat in the eggs.
3 Whisk the cream in a separate bowl until it forms soft peaks, then fold into the cream cheese mixture.

4 Scatter the blueberries evenly over the base of the prepared tin. Carefully pour the cheese mixture over the top. Cover the tin with a sheet of greaseproof paper and cook in the oven for 40-50 minutes, or until firm to the touch.
5 Allow to cool, then chill in the refrigerator until ready to serve.
6 To serve, unmould the cheesecake and place on the shortbread base. Dust with icing sugar.

SHORTBREAD

45 g (1½ oz) plain flour
20 g (¾ oz) caster sugar

30 g (1 oz) butter, softened

1 Combine the flour and sugar together in a bowl, then rub in the butter, using the fingertips. Mould together to give a soft dough.
2 Wrap in cling film and chill in the refrigerator for 15 minutes. Meanwhile preheat the oven to 200°C/400°F/Gas Mark 6.
3 Roll out the shortbread dough on a lightly floured surface to a 20 cm (8 inch) round,

approximately 5 mm (¼ inch) thick.
4 Transfer to a baking sheet, prick with a fork and bake in the oven for about 10 minutes until golden.

NOTE: This makes one 20 cm (8 inch) round. For individual rounds, cut four 8-10 cm (3¼-4 inch) rounds and bake for 8-10 minutes.

PLUM AND APRICOT PIE

SERVES 4-6

225 g (7½ oz) plain flour
1 tsp baking powder
½ tsp salt
120 g (4 oz) unsalted butter, diced
100 g (3½ oz) caster sugar
finely grated zest of 1 lemon

1 egg, beaten
250 g (8½ oz) plums, halved and stoned
250 g (8½ oz) apricots, halved and stoned
a little egg white, to glaze
TO SERVE
Raspberry Coulis (see page 16)

1 Sift the flour, baking powder and salt together into a bowl. Rub in the butter until the mixture resembles breadcrumbs. Add all but 1 tbsp of the sugar, the lemon zest and egg. Mix together to form a smooth dough. Wrap in cling film and chill in the refrigerator for 1 hour.

2 Roll out two thirds of the dough on a lightly floured surface to a 5 mm (¼ inch) thickness and use to line a buttered 15 cm (6 inch) loose-bottomed flan tin (or flan ring placed on a baking sheet).

3 Spoon the fruit into the pastry case, packing it in tightly and pressing firmly into the dough.

4 Roll out the remaining dough to a round, slightly larger than the diameter of the flan tin. Lay it over the fruit, then press the edge down the inside of the tin to seal. Chill in the refrigerator for 20 minutes. Meanwhile, preheat the oven to 190°C/375°F/Gas Mark 5.

5 Brush the top of the pie with egg white and sprinkle with the reserved 1 tbsp sugar. Bake for 25-30 minutes or until the pastry is golden brown.

6 Allow it to cool slightly, then remove from the tin. Cut the pie into wedges and serve with the raspberry coulis.

STRAWBERRY TARTLETS

SERVES 4

3 sheets of filo pastry

20 g (¾ oz) unsalted butter, melted

½ quantity Frangipane (see page 87)

2 tsp crème de framboise liqueur (optional)

4 tbsp pastry cream (see page 84), or whipped cream

14 medium strawberries, hulled

TO GLAZE

4 tbsp strawberry jam, warmed and sieved

TO DECORATE

few pistachio nuts, skinned and chopped

1 Preheat oven to 200°C/400°F/Gas Mark 6. Brush one sheet of filo pastry with melted butter. Lay another sheet on top and brush with more butter, then add the final filo sheet and brush again.

2 Cut out four 9-10 cm (3½-4 inch) rounds and use to line four 7.5 cm (3 inch) tartlet tins.

3 Divide the frangipane between the pastry cases and bake for about 10 minutes, until golden. Leave to cool.

4 If using the framboise liqueur, stir into the pastry cream or whipped cream. Spoon the cream into the centre of each tartlet, keeping it away from the edges or it will flow out when the fruit is pressed on.

5 Place a whole strawberry in the centre of each tart. Halve the rest of the strawberries and arrange around the whole ones. Brush with warm strawberry jam to glaze, then sprinkle a few chopped pistachios on top.

Bitter Chocolate Cappuccino Mousse (page 58); Chocolate Layers with Orange Mascarpone Sorbet and Summer Fruits

CHOCOLATE LAYERS WITH ORANGE MASCARPONE SORBET AND SUMMER FRUITS

SERVES 4

The combination of orange mascarpone sorbet and chocolate is a marriage made in heaven!

1 quantity Orange Mascarpone Sorbet
(see page 66)
FOR THE CHOCOLATE DISCS
90 g (3 oz) dark chocolate
45 g (1½ oz) white chocolate
FOR THE ORANGE COULIS
juice of 3 oranges
2 tsp cornflour

2 tbsp Grand Marnier
a little sugar (optional)
TO SERVE
8 sugar-dipped strawberries
16 raspberries
20 blueberries
few blackberries (optional)

1 From the sorbet, shape 8 discs, about 5 cm (2 inches) in diameter and 1 cm (½ inch) high. Place on a tray and freeze until firm.

2 To make the chocolate discs, melt the dark and white chocolate separately in heatproof bowls over hot water and stir until smooth.

3 Firstly pour the white chocolate onto a sheet of non-stick baking parchment. Immediately pour the dark chocolate on top and spread out as thinly as possible, using a palette knife to swirl the two chocolates together and create a marbled effect.

4 Leave until the chocolate is set, but still pliable, then cut out 12 discs, using a 6 cm (2½ inch) plain cutter. Leave until set hard, then

carefully peel away the paper.

5 To make the orange coulis, mix 1 tbsp of the orange juice with the cornflour until smooth. Bring the remaining orange juice to the boil in a saucepan, stir in the cornflour and cook, stirring, for 1-2 minutes until slightly thickened. Remove from the heat and stir in the liqueur, and a little sugar to taste if required. Allow to cool.

6 To assemble, lay a chocolate disc on each serving plate and position a disc of sorbet on top. Repeat these layers and top with the remaining chocolate discs. Surround with the orange coulis and decorate with the sugar-dipped strawberries and fresh berries.

BITTER CHOCOLATE CAPPUCCINO MOUSSE

SERVES 4

60 ml (2 fl oz) cappuccino coffee
200 g (7 oz) bitter chocolate, in pieces
120 g (4 oz) butter
2 egg yolks

3 egg whites
15 g (½ oz) caster sugar
60 ml (2 fl oz) Chocolate Sauce (see below)

1 Boil the cappuccino coffee in a saucepan to reduce by half. Let cool slightly.
2 Meanwhile, put the chocolate and butter in a small heatproof bowl over a pan of simmering water until melted; stir until smooth.
3 Add the cappuccino reduction and allow to cool until lukewarm, stirring continuously.
4 Add the egg yolks to the coffee and chocolate mixture and stir until smooth.
5 In a separate bowl, whisk the egg whites until they form soft peaks, then whisk in the sugar.
6 Stir one third of the egg whites into the chocolate mousse to lighten it, then gently fold the chocolate mousse into the remaining egg whites, using a metal spoon, until evenly incorporated.
7 Spoon into serving glasses and place in the refrigerator for 1 hour until set.
8 Spoon a little chocolate sauce onto each mousse to serve.

CHOCOLATE SAUCE

100 g (3½ oz) cocoa powder
300 ml (½ pint) water

225 g (8 oz) caster sugar
50 g (1¾ oz) plain chocolate, in pieces

1 Mix the cocoa powder to a paste with a little of the water. Put the sugar and remaining water in a small heavy-based pan and dissolve over a low heat.
2 Stir in the cocoa paste and chocolate. Bring to the boil, stirring constantly until the chocolate is melted and the sauce is smooth. Pass through a fine sieve into a bowl.

ROLLED ALMOND BISCUITS WITH CHOCOLATE MOUSSE AND ORANGE SAUCE

SERVES 4

This is definitely a dessert for chocolate lovers! Always prepare more than you think necessary as your guests are likely to want a second helping.

FOR THE BISCUITS
120 g (4 oz) plain flour
120 g (4 oz) caster sugar
3 egg whites (size 3)
45 g (1½ oz) butter, softened
60 g (2 oz) flaked almonds, toasted

TO ASSEMBLE
½ quantity Bitter Chocolate Cappuccino Mousse (see left)
100 g (3½ oz) apricot jam
300 ml (½ pint) orange juice

1 Preheat oven to 180°C/350°F/Gas Mark 4. Chill 2 greased baking sheets in the refrigerator.
2 Mix the flour, sugar and egg whites together in a bowl. Add the softened butter and mix until smooth.
3 Place 12 heaped teaspoonfuls of the mixture on the baking sheets, spacing them well apart; spread out thinly to 7 cm (2¾ inch) rounds with the back of a spoon. (Alternately spread a little of the mixture thinly in 7 cm (2¾ inch) plastic stencils; remove the stencil and repeat until all the mixture is used up.) You should have enough for 12 biscuits. Sprinkle the flaked almonds over the biscuits.
4 Bake one sheet at a time, for 5-8 minutes until the edges of the biscuits turn golden. Using a palette knife, carefully lift the biscuits

off the tray and immediately wrap each one around the handle of a wooden spoon, pressing firmly. Once set, carefully slide the biscuits off the handles.
5 Using a piping bag fitted with a small plain nozzle, fill the ends of the biscuits with the chocolate mousse.
6 Purée the apricot jam and orange juice together in a blender, then pass through a fine sieve into a bowl.
7 Arrange 3 biscuits on each serving plate and surround with the apricot and orange sauce. Serve immediately.

NOTE: If the biscuits harden before you have time to shape them, return the baking sheet to the oven for 30 seconds or so.

RASPBERRY CREAM GÂTEAU

SERVES 10

Cream gâteaux invariably bring back memories of my childhood and I still love the flavour of fresh soft fruit sandwiched between moistened sponge and whipped cream.

FOR THE GENOESE SPONGE
4 eggs
120 g (4 oz) caster sugar
120 g (4 oz) plain flour
20 g (¾ oz) butter, melted and cooled
FOR THE FILLING
90 ml (3 fl oz) sugar syrup (see page 86)
50 ml (2 fl oz) Cointreau

600 ml (1 pint) double cream
2 tbsp icing sugar
few drops of vanilla essence
60 g (2 oz) raspberry jam
350 g (12 oz) raspberries
150 g (5 oz) flaked almonds, toasted
1 tsp pistachio nuts, skinned and chopped

1 Grease and line a 20 cm (8 inch) round cake tin. Preheat the oven to 180°C/350°F/Gas Mark 4.

2 Put the eggs and sugar in a heatproof bowl set over a pan of simmering water and whisk, using a hand-held electric mixer, until the mixture is pale, thick and substantially increased in volume. Remove the bowl from the pan and continue to whisk until the mixture is cool.

3 Sift the flour over the mixture and fold in carefully, using a large metal spoon. Pour the melted butter around the edge of the mixture and, again, fold in carefully.

4 Pour the sponge mixture into the prepared tin and bake in the oven for 30–35 minutes, until risen and firm to the touch. Turn out onto a wire rack and leave to cool.

5 When cold, carefully slice the sponge horizontally into 3 layers. Mix the sugar syrup with the Cointreau and sprinkle evenly over the sponge layers.

6 Whip the cream with the icing sugar and vanilla essence until it holds its shape. Place one sponge layer on a serving plate and spread with the raspberry jam. Cover with a layer of whipped cream and half of the raspberries. Position a second sponge layer on top and spread with whipped cream. Cover with the third sponge layer. Spread the remaining cream over the top and side of the gâteau.

7 Press the toasted flaked almonds around the side of the gâteau and arrange the rest of the raspberries on the top. Sprinkle with the chopped pistachio nuts to finish.

Raspberry Cream Gâteau

STRAWBERRY DOME

SERVES 4

FOR THE SPONGE
4 eggs, separated
60 g (2 oz) caster sugar
65 g (2¼ oz) plain flour
TO ASSEMBLE
150 g (5 oz) strawberry jam
320 g (11 oz) strawberries, quartered
20 g (¾ oz) caster sugar

60 ml (2 fl oz) Grand Marnier
60 ml (2 fl oz) sherry
1 gelatine leaf
60 g (2 oz) apricot jam, warmed and sieved
TO DECORATE
4 strawberries (on stems)

1 Draw a 16 cm (6½ inch) square on a sheet of non-stick baking parchment, then invert onto a baking sheet. Preheat the oven to 220°C/425°F/ Gas Mark 7.

2 Whisk the egg yolks with 20 g (¾ oz) of the sugar until pale and creamy.

3 Whisk the egg whites in a separate bowl until they form stiff peaks. Gradually whisk in the remaining sugar, a spoonful at a time, to make a stiff, glossy meringue.

4 Fold the meringue into the egg yolk mixture, then sift the flour over the mixture and carefully fold in.

5 Spread the sponge mixture evenly over the marked square. Bake in the oven for 12-14 minutes until risen and just firm to the touch.

6 Spread the sponge with the strawberry jam and roll up tightly. Let cool, then place in the freezer for about 45 minutes until firm.

7 Meanwhile, put the strawberries in a shallow dish and sprinkle with the sugar, Grand Marnier and sherry. Leave to stand for 30 minutes.

8 Cut the frozen sponge into 5 mm (¼ inch) slices. Line 4 small bowls, approximately 8 cm (3¼ inches) in diameter and 4-5 cm (1½-2 inches) deep, with the Swiss roll slices, placing them as closely together as possible.

9 Soak the gelatine leaf in cold water to cover for about 10 minutes to soften. Drain the soaking liquor from the strawberries into a small pan and bring to the boil. Remove from the heat. Squeeze excess water from the gelatine leaf, then add the leaf to the hot liquid, stirring until dissolved. Allow to cool until on the point of setting. Quickly dip the strawberries in and out of the setting liquor so that they are lightly covered with a layer of jelly.

10 Pack the strawberries firmly into the sponge-lined bowls and cover with a slice of the Swiss roll. Chill in the refrigerator for 2 hours.

11 To serve, turn out the strawberry domes onto individual serving plates and brush all over with the warm apricot jam to glaze. Decorate with strawberries.

VANILLA ICE CREAM

SERVES 4-6

200 ml (7 fl oz) milk

200 ml (7 fl oz) double cream

1 vanilla pod, split

6 egg yolks

75 g (2½ oz) caster sugar

3 tbsp liquid glucose

1 Put the milk and cream in a heavy-based saucepan. Scrape the seeds from the vanilla pod into the pan, and add the pod too. Slowly bring to the boil over a gentle heat.

2 Meanwhile, beat the egg yolks and sugar together in a bowl until pale and thick. Pour on the milk mixture, whisking until well blended, then return to the pan. Cook over a very gentle heat, stirring constantly, until the custard is thick enough to coat the back of the spoon; do not allow to boil or it will curdle.

3 Remove from the heat and pass through a fine sieve into a chilled bowl, then stir in the glucose. Cool as quickly as possible - ideally in the refrigerator.

4 Freeze the mixture in an ice-cream machine according to the manufacturer's instructions. Alternatively, pour into a large freezerproof bowl, cover and freeze until almost set. Transfer to a food processor and process until creamy and all the ice crystals are broken down. Put the mixture back into the bowl, cover and return to the freezer. Repeat this process twice, then freeze until firm.

WILD STRAWBERRY AND FROMAGE FRAIS ICE CREAM

SERVES 6

240 g (8 oz) wild strawberries

80 g (2¾ oz) icing sugar

300 g (10 oz) fromage frais

wild strawberries to decorate

1 Put the wild strawberries and icing sugar in a blender or food processor and work to a purée.

2 Pass through a fine sieve into a bowl and stir in the fromage frais.

3 Freeze the mixture as for Vanilla Ice Cream (see step 4, above).

4 Scoop the ice cream into glass dishes and decorate with strawberries to serve.

LEMON MASCARPONE ICE CREAM

SERVES 4

finely grated zest of ½ lemon
150 ml (¼ pint) lemon juice
3 egg yolks

125 g (4¼ oz) caster sugar
250 g (8½ oz) mascarpone cheese
lemon zest shreds to decorate

1 Put the lemon zest and juice into a small heavy-based saucepan and bring to the boil.
2 Meanwhile, beat the egg yolks and sugar together in a bowl, then pour on the lemon juice, stirring continuously.
3 Return to the pan and stir over a gentle heat until the mixture thickens slightly; do not allow to boil or it will curdle.
4 Pass through a fine sieve into a chilled bowl and allow to cool. Stir in the mascarpone.
5 Freeze in an ice-cream machine according to the manufacturer's instructions. Alternatively, pour into a large freezerproof bowl, cover and freeze until almost set. Whisk to break down the ice crystals, then cover and return to the freezer. Repeat this process twice.
6 Scoop into glass dishes and decorate with lemon zest shreds to serve.

GIN AND GRAPEFRUIT GRANITA

SERVES 6

250 ml (8 fl oz) grapefruit juice
juice of ½ lemon
240 g (8 oz) caster sugar

250 ml (8 fl oz) water
2 tbsp gin
mint sprigs to decorate

1 Put the grapefruit juice, lemon juice, sugar and water in a saucepan over a low heat until the sugar is dissolved, then bring to the boil and simmer for 45 seconds. Allow to cool.
2 Pass through a fine sieve into a bowl and add the gin. Pour the liquid into a shallow freezer-proof container, approximately 2 cm (¾ inch) deep, and carefully place in the freezer.
3 When the mixture is completely frozen into ice crystals it is ready to serve. Scrape up the ice crystals with a fork and transfer to chilled glasses. Decorate with mint and serve at once.

Gin and Grapefruit Granita; Lemon Mascarpone Ice Cream

ORANGE MASCARPONE SORBET

SERVES 8

110 g (3¾ oz) caster sugar
240 ml (7½ fl oz) water
180 g (6 oz) mascarpone

juice of ½ lemon
dash of rum
1 tbsp orange marmalade

1 Put the sugar and water in a saucepan and dissolve over a low heat, then bring to the boil. Set aside to cool completely.

2 Stir in the mascarpone cheese, lemon juice and rum.

3 Freeze in an ice-cream machine, according to the manufacturer's instructions, adding the orange marmalade when the ice cream is almost firm. Alternatively, pour the mixture into a large freezerproof bowl, cover and freeze until almost set. Transfer to a food processor and whizz to break down the ice crystals. Add the orange marmalade and process until evenly blended. Return to the bowl, cover and freeze for 3 hours or until almost set, then whizz again to ensure a fine-textured sorbet. Cover and freeze for 2 hours.

4 Just before serving, mash the sorbet well with a fork. Scoop into glass dishes to serve.

NOTE: If the sorbet has been left in the freezer for a while and frozen very hard, transfer it to the refrigerator 20-30 minutes before serving to soften slightly.

RASPBERRY SORBET

SERVES 6

60 g (2 oz) caster sugar
6 tbsp water

350 g (12 oz) raspberries
juice of 1 lemon

1 Put the sugar and water in a saucepan and dissolve over a low heat, then bring to the boil. Remove from the heat and set aside to cool completely.
2 Put the raspberries and lemon juice in a blender or food processor and work to a purée. Pass through a fine sieve into a bowl. Stir in the cooled sugar syrup.
3 Freeze the mixture in an ice-cream machine according to the manufacturer's instructions. Alternatively, pour the mixture into a large freezerproof bowl, cover and freeze until almost set. Transfer to a food processor and whizz to

break down the ice crystals. Return to the bowl, cover and freeze for 3 hours or until almost set, then repeat this process again to ensure a fine-textured sorbet. Cover and freeze for 2 hours.
4 Just before serving, mash the sorbet well with a fork. Scoop into glass dishes and decorate with raspberries to serve.

NOTE: If the sorbet has been left in the freezer for a while and frozen very hard, transfer it to the refrigerator 20-30 minutes before serving to soften slightly.

ELDERFLOWER SORBET

SERVES 6

15 g (½ oz) caster sugar
360 ml (12 fl oz) water

360 ml (12 fl oz) elderflower syrup

1 Put the sugar and water in a saucepan and dissolve over a low heat, then bring to the boil. Remove from the heat and add the elderflower syrup. Set aside to cool completely.
2 Freeze the elderflower syrup mixture as for

Raspberry Sorbet (see step 3, above).
3 Scoop the sorbet into glass dishes to serve.

NOTE: If the sorbet has frozen hard, place in the refrigerator 20-30 minutes before serving.

Autumn

Apple Pudding

Steamed Chocolate Pudding
with Minted Custard Sauce

Prune and Armagnac Soufflé

Prune Clafoutis

Apple Pancakes

Mirabelle Dumplings

Damson Fritters on Cherry Compote

Apple Jack Pie with a Cheddar Crumble

Glazed Poached Pears filled with Mascarpone

Diana's Exotic Fruit Gratinée

Hazelnut Tart

Apple Upside-down Tarts with Vanilla Sauce

Plum Tarts with Sabayon

Tarte Bourdaloue

Pear Frangipane Tartlets

Caramelized Pears with Brandy Snap Baskets
and Vanilla Ice Cream

Walnut Tart

Lemon and Passion Fruit Tart

Fig and Raspberry Royale

Damson Compote with Clotted Cream

Granny Smith Sorbet

Opera Chocolate Slice

Chocolate Gâteau with Grand Marnier

APPLE PUDDING

SERVES 4

10 thin slices of white bread, crusts removed
200 g (7 oz) butter
4 cooking apples
40 g (1¼ oz) light brown sugar

juice of ½ lemon
1 clove
TO SERVE
apricot conserve, warmed
dash of brandy or rum

1 Preheat oven to 200°C/400°F/Gas Mark 6. Cut four 3 cm (1¼ inch) circles from one of the slices of bread; set aside. Cut the rest of the slices into triangular pieces.
2 Melt 160 g (5½ oz) of the butter. Dip the bread triangles into the melted butter, then use to line 4 dariole moulds, overlapping them slightly.
3 Dip the bread circles into the remaining melted butter and use to line the base of the moulds.
4 Peel, core and slice the apples. Melt the remaining 40 g (1½ oz) butter in a saucepan.

Add the apples, sugar, lemon juice and clove. Cook gently for about 10 minutes until the apples are softened and reduced. Discard the clove. Let cool.
5 Fill the prepared moulds with the stewed apple. Bake in the oven for 25 minutes.
6 Turn the puddings out onto warmed serving plates and serve with the warm apricot conserve, flavoured with a dash of brandy or rum.

NOTE: The bread should look toasted and golden when the puddings are turned out.

STEAMED CHOCOLATE PUDDING

SERVES 4

150 g (5 oz) good-quality plain chocolate
15 g (½ oz) unsalted butter
3 eggs, separated
3 tbsp caster sugar

TO SERVE
icing sugar for dusting
Minted Custard Sauce (see below)

1 Melt the chocolate with the butter in a large heatproof bowl over a pan of simmering water. Remove from the heat, let cool slightly, then beat in the egg yolks.
2 In a large clean bowl, whisk the egg whites until stiff peaks form, then gradually whisk in the sugar. Stir a spoonful of the whites into the chocolate mixture to loosen it, then carefully fold in the remaining whites with a metal spoon. Cover and refrigerate for 1½-2 hours.
3 Preheat oven to 200°C/400°F/Gas Mark 6.

Generously butter 4 ramekins, 8 cm (3¼ inches) in diameter.
4 Divide the chocolate mixture between the ramekins and bake in the oven for 15 minutes or until risen. Remove from the oven and leave to rest in a warm place for 15 minutes.
5 Loosen each pudding with a small sharp knife, then turn it out into your hand. Set each pudding upright in the centre of a warmed serving plate and dust lightly with icing sugar. Serve with the minted custard sauce.

MINTED CUSTARD SAUCE

400 ml (14 fl oz) milk
1 vanilla pod, split
7 egg yolks

80 g (2¾ oz) caster sugar
2 tbsp finely chopped fresh mint

1 Put the milk and vanilla pod in a heavy-based saucepan. Bring slowly to just below the boil, then remove from the heat and set aside to infuse for 10 minutes.
2 Meanwhile, whisk the egg yolks and sugar together in a bowl until pale. Bring the milk to just below a simmer, then gradually pour onto

the egg mixture, stirring constantly.
3 Return to the pan and cook over low heat, stirring constantly, with a wooden spoon, until the sauce thickens enough to thinly coat the back of the spoon.
4 Strain the sauce through a fine sieve into a chilled bowl. Stir in the freshly chopped mint.

Prune and Armagnac Soufflé

PRUNE AND ARMAGNAC SOUFFLÉ

SERVES 4

Prunes and armagnac is a terrific combination with a superb strong depth of flavour.

12 prunes, stoned and chopped	3 eggs, separated
3 tbsp armagnac	45 g (1½ oz) caster sugar
180 ml (6 fl oz) milk	TO SERVE
30 g (1 oz) plain flour	Vanilla Sauce (see page 83)
30 g (1 oz) butter	

1 Preheat oven to 425°C/220°F/Gas Mark 7. Put the prunes in a small bowl, sprinkle with the armagnac and leave to soak for 20 minutes.
2 Generously butter 4 individual soufflé dishes, about 8 cm (3¼ inches) in diameter, then sprinkle with sugar.
3 Bring the milk to the boil in a saucepan. Meanwhile mix the flour and butter to a paste to form a beurre manié. Add the beurre manié to the hot milk, a small piece at a time, whisking all the time. Bring back to the boil and cook, stirring, until thickened and smooth. Remove from the heat.
4 Beat in the egg yolks, one at a time. Stir in the prunes and armagnac. Allow to cool, until lukewarm.
5 In another large clean bowl, whisk the egg whites until stiff, then whisk in the sugar, until the meringue forms firm peaks. Stir a spoonful of the meringue into the prune mixture to loosen it, then gently fold in the rest of the meringue.
6 Divide the mixture between the prepared soufflé dishes, to three-quarters fill them. Stand the dishes in a bain-marie (or roasting tin containing enough water to come halfway up the sides of the dishes). Bake in the oven for about 15-20 minutes until well risen and slightly firm.
7 Remove the soufflés from the bain-marie and loosen the sides with a small sharp knife. Turn each one out onto the centre of a warmed serving plate. Pour the vanilla sauce around the soufflés and serve immediately.

PRUNE CLAFOUTIS

SERVES 4-6

120 g (4 oz) prunes, stoned
3 tbsp armagnac
100 ml (3½ fl oz) milk
150 ml (¼ pint) double cream
4 eggs

120 g (4 oz) caster sugar
15 g (½ oz) plain flour, sifted
20 g (¾ oz) ground almonds
icing sugar for dusting

1 Preheat oven to 180°C/350°F/Gas Mark 4. Put the prunes in a small bowl, sprinkle with the armagnac and leave to soak for 20 minutes.
2 Pour the milk and cream into a saucepan and slowly bring to the boil.
3 Meanwhile whisk the eggs and sugar together in a bowl until pale and creamy. Add the flour and ground almonds and whisk thoroughly until the mixture is smooth.

4 Slowly pour on the hot milk and cream mixture, whisking all the time, until smooth.
5 Scatter the prunes and armagnac over the base of a greased and floured 20 cm (8 inch) shallow ovenproof dish. Pour the creamy batter over the top.
6 Bake in the oven for 30-35 minutes, until set and golden. Allow to cool slightly.
7 Serve warm, dusted with icing sugar.

APPLE PANCAKES

SERVES 4

100 g (3½ oz) unsalted butter
2 eggs
250 ml (8 fl oz) milk
100 g (3½ oz) caster sugar

140 g (4½ oz) plain flour
pinch of salt
4 Golden Delicious apples, cored
icing sugar for dusting

1 Melt 20 g (¾ oz) of the butter in a pan and heat it until it turns golden brown. Pass through a fine sieve into a small bowl.
2 Whisk the eggs, milk and 60 g (2 oz) of the sugar together in a bowl.

3 Sift the flour and salt into another bowl, then whisk in the egg mixture and the browned butter until smooth.
4 Slice each apple into 6-8 rings. Melt a quarter of the remaining butter in a large crêpe pan.

Add a quarter of the apple rings and sprinkle with a quarter of the remaining sugar. Cook for about 3 minutes on each side, until soft and caramelized.

5 Pour a quarter of the batter over the apples and cook over a low heat for 2-3 minutes, until set. Slide on to a baking sheet, place the pan on top and invert the pancake back into the pan. Cook for 2 minutes, until golden brown.

6 Slide the pancake onto a plate and keep warm, while you make 3 more pancakes in the same way. Serve dusted with icing sugar.

MIRABELLE DUMPLINGS

SERVES 4

A scrumptious pudding, but not one for weight-watchers! The season for mirabelles is quite short, but plums work equally well.

250 g (8½ oz) potatoes, peeled and quartered
25 g (¾ oz) semolina
50 g (1¾ oz) self-raising flour
1 small egg (size 4 or 5)

75 g (2½ oz) butter, softened (approximately)
16 mirabelle plums, stoned
120 g (4 oz) soft white breadcrumbs
icing sugar for dusting

1 Cook the potatoes in unsalted boiling water until tender, drain well and mash smoothly. Allow to cool.

2 Place the cooled, mashed potatoes in a food processor with the semolina, flour, egg and 50 g (1¾ oz) of the butter. Work to a smooth dough.

3 Turn onto a floured surface, knead lightly and roll out to a large square, 5 mm (¼ inch) thick. Cut the dough into sixteen 5 cm (2 inch) squares. Place a mirabelle in the centre of each square and gather up the edges over the top; twist and press together to seal.

4 Bring a large pan of salted water to the boil. Lower 4-5 dumplings into the water and simmer for about 2 minutes until they rise to the surface. Remove with a slotted spoon and drain on kitchen paper; keep warm while cooking the rest of the dumplings.

5 Melt the remaining butter in a frying pan. Add the breadcrumbs and fry, stirring, until golden. (If too dry, add a little more butter.) Spread the breadcrumbs on a plate.

6 Gently roll the dumplings in the breadcrumbs to coat. Dust with icing sugar and serve.

DAMSON FRITTERS ON CHERRY COMPOTE

SERVES 4-6

FOR THE CHERRY COMPOTE

juice of 1 orange

200 ml (7 fl oz) water

60 g (2 oz) caster sugar

300 g (10 oz) ripe cherries, stoned

1 cinnamon stick

2 tbsp kirsch

2 tbsp cornflour

FOR THE DAMSON FRITTERS

180 g (6 oz) plain flour

200 ml (7 fl oz) white wine

3 egg yolks

few drops of vanilla essence

½ tsp finely grated lemon zest

1 tbsp brandy

50 g (1¾ oz) marzipan

20 damsons

vegetable oil for deep-frying

TO SERVE

caster sugar for sprinkling

pinch of ground cinnamon

mint sprigs to decorate

1 To prepare the compote, put the orange juice, water and sugar into a saucepan over a low heat until the sugar is dissolved, then bring to the boil. Add the cherries, cinnamon stick and kirsch and bring to a simmer.

2 Meanwhile, mix the cornflour with a little cold water to a smooth paste, then stir into the cherry compote. Cook, stirring, for a few minutes until slightly thickened. Remove from the heat and allow to cool.

3 To make the fritter batter, sift the flour into a bowl, then gradually beat in the wine to make a smooth batter. Cover and leave to stand in a cool place for 20 minutes.

4 Add the egg yolks, vanilla essence and lemon zest to the batter; mix until smooth. If there are any lumps, pass through a fine sieve into a clean bowl.

5 Knead the brandy into the marzipan. Make a slit in the side of each damson and carefully remove the stone. Stuff the damsons with the brandy-flavoured marzipan.

6 Heat the oil in a deep-fryer to 190°C (375°F). Dip the stuffed damsons into the fritter batter to coat, then deep-fry in the hot oil for 2-3 minutes until golden brown. Drain on kitchen paper.

7 To serve, roll the damson fritters in the sugar mixed with the cinnamon to coat. Divide the warm cherry compote between individual serving bowls and arrange the damson fritters on top. Decorate with mint sprigs.

Damson Fritters on Cherry Compote

APPLE JACK PIE WITH A CHEDDAR CRUMBLE

SERVES 6-8

250 g (8½ oz) Sweet Pastry (see page 15)
8 Cox's apples
30 g (1 oz) butter
30 g (1 oz) sugar
2 tbsp treacle
90 g (3 oz) sultanas

FOR THE CRUMBLE
240 g (8 oz) plain flour
120 g (4 oz) butter
90 g (3 oz) caster sugar
90 g (3 oz) Cheddar or Red Leicester
cheese, grated

1 Roll out the sweet pastry on a lightly floured surface to a 3 mm (⅛ inch) thickness and use to line a deep 20 cm (8 inch) loose-bottomed flan tin (or flan ring placed on a baking sheet). Chill in the refrigerator for 20 minutes. Meanwhile, preheat the oven to 180°C/350°F/Gas Mark 4.
2 Quarter, peel, core and slice the apples. Melt the butter in a pan, add the apples with the sugar and cook gently for about 10 minutes until softened.

3 Remove from the heat, add the treacle and sultanas, and allow to cool. Fill the pastry case with the apples.
4 For the crumble, sift the flour into a bowl. Rub in the butter until the mixture resembles breadcrumbs, then stir in the sugar and gently incorporate the cheese.
5 Spoon the crumble over the apples and bake in the oven for about 25 minutes until the crumble topping is golden.

GLAZED POACHED PEARS FILLED WITH MASCARPONE

SERVES 4

Pears, mascarpone and almonds go together extremely well in this delightful dish. It can also be made with apricots and peaches.

400 g (14 oz) caster sugar
500 ml (16 fl oz) water
1 vanilla pod, split
4 firm, ripe pears (preferably Comice)
30 g (1 oz) mascarpone cheese
100 g (3½ oz) flaked almonds

FOR THE SABAYON
125 ml (4 fl oz) double cream
120 g (4 oz) mascarpone cheese
3 tbsp brandy
1 tsp lemon juice
2 egg yolks
45 g (1½ oz) caster sugar

1 Put the sugar and water in a medium saucepan with the split vanilla pod. Heat gently, stirring to dissolve the sugar, then bring to the boil and simmer for 1 minute.

2 Peel the pears, then scoop out the core from the base of each one. Add the pears to the syrup and poach for 40-50 minutes, depending on ripeness, until just tender. Drain.

3 Using a piping bag fitted with a small nozzle, pipe the mascarpone into each pear to fill the hollow left by the core. Arrange the pears in a flameproof serving dish and chill until ready to serve.

4 Spread the almonds on a baking sheet and toast under a preheated high grill for 1 minute or until turning golden, shaking occasionally to ensure they colour evenly. Set aside.

5 To make the sabayon, whip the cream in a bowl until beginning to thicken. Add the mascarpone and continue whipping until the mixture is thick but not stiff; set aside.

6 Put the brandy and lemon juice in a small pan and bring to the boil.

7 Place the egg yolks and sugar in a large heat-proof bowl set over a pan of gently simmering water and whisk until the mixture is pale, thick and substantially increased in volume.

8 Remove the bowl from the pan and whisk in the brandy mixture. Continue whisking until the mixture is cold. Carefully fold in the mascarpone cream.

9 Cover the pears with the mascarpone sabayon and sprinkle the toasted almonds on top. Place under a preheated high grill for about 30 seconds, just until the surface is glazed and lightly coloured. Serve immediately.

DIANA'S EXOTIC FRUIT GRATINÉE

SERVES 4

An incredibly quick dessert which has maximum visual impact! You can, of course, use other fruit, such as blackberries, blueberries, strawberries and raspberries if you prefer.

3 egg yolks
45 g (1½ oz) caster sugar
3 tbsp eau de vie de framboises
4 tbsp double cream
½ mango, peeled, and cut into 1 cm (¾ inch) cubes

½ paw-paw, peeled and cut into 1 cm (¾ inch) cubes
1 kiwi fruit, peeled and cut into 1 cm (¾ inch) cubes
1 banana, peeled and sliced

1 Put the egg yolks, sugar and framboise in a heatproof bowl over a pan of simmering water and whisk until the mixture has trebled in volume, to form a light, foamy sabayon.
2 Remove from the heat and continue whisking until the sabayon is cold.

3 Whip the cream lightly until beginning to thicken, then fold into the sabayon.
4 Divide the fruit between 4 individual gratin dishes and spoon on the sabayon to cover. Place under a preheated hot grill for 1–2 minutes until golden brown. Serve at once.

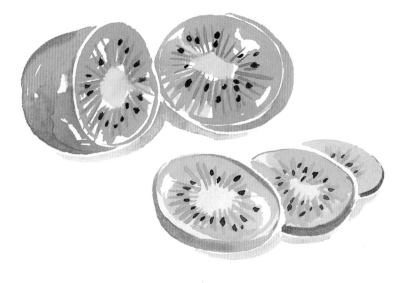

Exotic Fruit Gratinée

HAZELNUT TART

SERVES 6-8

250 g (8½ oz) Sweet Pastry (see page 15)
300 g (10 oz) shelled hazelnuts
3 eggs

150 g (5 oz) soft brown sugar
75 g (2½ oz) unsalted butter, melted
100 g (3½ oz) golden syrup

1 Preheat oven to 170°C/325°F/Gas Mark 3. Roll out the pastry thinly on a lightly floured surface and use to line a deep 20 cm (8 inch) flan tin.
2 Set aside 50 g (2 oz) of the hazelnuts. Place the rest in a food processor with the eggs, sugar, melted butter and syrup. Process briefly, until the mixture is evenly blended and the nuts are coarsely chopped.
3 Pour the mixture into the pastry case and arrange the reserved hazelnuts on top. Bake for 40-50 minutes, until the filling is set.

APPLE UPSIDE-DOWN TARTS

SERVES 4

100 g (3½ oz) caster sugar
400 ml (14 fl oz) water
1 tbsp liquid glucose
7 medium dessert apples
juice of ½ lemon

ground cinnamon for sprinkling
50 g (1¾ oz) unsalted butter
100 g (3½ oz) puff pastry
Vanilla Sauce (see below) to serve
mint sprigs to decorate

1 Preheat oven to 180°C/350°F/Gas Mark 4. Put the sugar, water and glucose in a heavy-based saucepan over a low heat until the sugar is dissolved, then increase the heat and cook to a pale amber coloured caramel.

2 Put a little of this caramel into each of 4 ramekins, about 9 cm (3½ inches) in diameter and 4 cm (1½ inches) high, tilting the dishes to ensure the caramel coats the bases.

3 Peel, core and thinly slice the apples; immediately sprinkle with the lemon juice and a little cinnamon.

4 Fill the ramekins with apple slices and bake for 15 minutes until soft and reduced.

5 Meanwhile, sauté the remaining apple slices in the butter until soft. Top up the ramekin dishes with this mixture and leave to cool. Increase the oven setting to 190°C/375°F/Gas Mark 5.

6 Roll out the puff pastry on a lightly floured surface to a 3 mm (½ inch) thickness and cut out four rounds, slightly larger than the ramekins. Prick all over with a fork and leave to rest in a cool place for 20 minutes.

7 Cover the ramekins with the puff pastry rounds and bake for 20 minutes.

8 Leave to cool slightly before turning each one out on to a serving plate. Surround with the warm vanilla sauce and decorate with mint.

VANILLA SAUCE

500 ml (16 fl oz) milk
1 vanilla pod, split

6 egg yolks
75 g (2½ oz) caster sugar

1 Put the milk and vanilla pod in a heavy-based saucepan. Bring slowly to just below the boil, then set aside to infuse for 10 minutes.

2 Whisk the egg yolks and sugar together in a bowl until pale. Bring the milk to the boil, then pour on to the egg yolk mixture, whisking.

3 Return the mixture to the cleaned pan and stir gently over a low heat, using a wooden spoon, until the sauce thickens enough to thinly coat the back of the spoon; do not allow to boil or it will curdle. Pass the sauce through a fine sieve into a bowl.

PLUM TARTS WITH SABAYON

SERVES 4

200 g (7 oz) puff pastry
4 tbsp Pastry Cream (see below)
300 g (10 oz) plums, halved, stoned and thinly sliced
20 g (¾ oz) plain flour
15 g (½ oz) soft brown sugar
15 g (½ oz) hazelnuts, chopped
large pinch of ground cinnamon

15 g (½ oz) unsalted butter, melted
FOR THE SABAYON
5 egg yolks
75 g (2½ oz) caster sugar
100 ml (3½ fl oz) Sauternes
50 ml (3 tbsp) lemon juice
50 ml (3 tbsp) orange juice

1 Roll out the puff pastry thinly on a lightly floured surface to about a 3 mm (⅛ inch) thickness and cut out four 12 cm (5 inch) rounds. Place on a large buttered baking sheet, prick all over with a fork and leave to rest in the refrigerator for 30 minutes.
2 Preheat oven to 200°C/400°F/Gas Mark 6. Spread a thin layer of pastry cream over each pastry round. Arrange the plum slices on top.
3 Mix the flour, sugar, hazelnuts, cinnamon and butter together. Sprinkle over the plums. Bake for 15-20 minutes until golden brown.
4 For the sabayon, put the egg yolks, caster sugar, Sauternes, and lemon and orange juices in a heatproof bowl. Set over a pan of boiling water and whisk, using a hand-held electric mixer, until the mixture is tripled in volume and forms a light, fluffy sabayon.
5 To serve, place the tartlets on warmed serving plates and serve with the warm sabayon.

PASTRY CREAM

150 ml (¼ pint) milk
½ vanilla pod, split
1 egg yolk

20 g (¾ oz) caster sugar
20 g (¾ oz) plain flour, sifted

1 Put the milk in a small heavy-based pan. Scrape out the seeds from the vanilla pod and add to the milk, together with the pod. Slowly bring to the boil over a gentle heat.
2 Meanwhile, whisk the egg yolk and sugar together in a bowl until pale and creamy. Add the flour and mix to a smooth paste. Pour on half of the boiling milk, whisking until smooth.
3 Return to the pan and stir in the remaining milk. Bring to the boil, stirring constantly, and cook for 1-2 minutes until thickened. Pass through a fine sieve into a bowl. Allow to cool.

Tarte Bourdaloue (page 86); Plum Tarts with Sabayon

TARTE BOURDALOUE

SERVES 8

200 g (7 oz) Sweet Pastry (see page 15)
100 g (3½ oz) ground almonds
25 g (¾ oz) plain flour
100 g (3½ oz) caster sugar
100 ml (3½ fl oz) egg white
25 g (¾ oz) unsalted butter
50 ml (3 tbsp) Poire William liqueur
1 litre (1¾ pints) Sugar Syrup (see below)

4 small pears, peeled and cored
TO FINISH
2-3 tbsp apricot jam, warmed and sieved, to glaze
icing sugar for dusting
TO SERVE
Vanilla Sauce (see page 83)

1 Roll out the sweet pastry on a lightly floured surface to a 3 mm (⅛ inch) thickness and use to line a 20 cm (8 inch) loose-bottomed flan tin (or flan ring placed on a baking sheet). Chill in the refrigerator for 20 minutes. Meanwhile, pre-heat the oven to 180°C/350°F/Gas Mark 4.
2 Mix the ground almonds, flour, sugar and egg white together in a bowl until smooth. Melt the butter in a small pan over a high heat until it turns nut brown in colour, then quickly stir into the almond mixture. Stir in the Poire William liqueur.
3 Heat the sugar syrup in a saucepan, add the

pears and poach until just tender. Leave to cool in the syrup, then drain well and halve lengthwise.
4 Spread the almond mixture evenly over the base of the flan case. Arrange the pear halves, curved surface uppermost, on top.
5 Bake in the oven for about 45 minutes until golden brown and just firm.
6 Remove the flan from the tin and lightly brush the surface with warm apricot jam to glaze. Dust the edge of the flan with icing sugar. Serve immediately, accompanied by the warm vanilla sauce.

SUGAR SYRUP

500 g (1 lb 2 oz) caster sugar
1 litre (1¾ pints) water

3 tbsp lemon juice

Put the sugar and water in a saucepan; dissolve over a low heat. Add the lemon juice and bring to the boil. Boil for 1 minute, then leave to

cool. Strain and use as required. The syrup will keep in the refrigerator for 1-2 weeks. Makes about 1 litre (1¾ pints).

PEAR FRANGIPANE TARTLETS

SERVES 4

250 g (8½ oz) caster sugar
500 ml (16 fl oz) water
few drops of lemon juice
1 cinnamon stick
½ vanilla pod
1 large pear, peeled, quartered and cored

120 g (4 oz) Sweet Pastry (see page 15)
4 tsp raspberry jam
1 quantity Frangipane (see below)
TO GLAZE
4 tbsp apricot jam, warmed and sieved

1 Preheat oven to 200°C/400°F/Gas Mark 6. Put the sugar and water in a saucepan and heat gently until the sugar has dissolved, then add the lemon juice, cinnamon stick and vanilla pod and bring to the boil.
2 Add the pear quarters to the syrup and simmer gently until just tender.
3 Remove the pears from the syrup and leave to cool, then slice each pear quarter lengthwise, leaving the slices attached at the stalk end, so they can be fanned out.

4 Roll out the pastry on a lightly floured surface to a 3 mm (⅛ inch) thickness. Cut out four 11–12 cm (4½–5 inch) rounds and use to line 4 deep 7.5 cm (3 inch) tartlet tins.
5 Place a teaspoon of raspberry jam in each pastry case. Divide the frangipane between them, then top each with a pear fan.
6 Bake in the oven for about 20 minutes, until the frangipane is golden brown. Leave to cool slightly, then brush with the warm apricot jam to glaze.

FRANGIPANE

30 g (1 oz) unsalted butter
30 g (1 oz) caster sugar
2 tbsp beaten egg

30 g (1 oz) ground almonds
1 tbsp plain flour, sifted

Cream the butter and sugar together until pale, using an electric mixer. Gradually beat in the egg until evenly incorporated, then fold in the ground almonds and flour.

Caramelized Pears with Brandy Snap Baskets and Vanilla Ice Cream

CARAMELIZED PEARS WITH BRANDY SNAP BASKETS AND VANILLA ICE CREAM

SERVES 4

BRANDY SNAP BASKETS
30 g (1 oz) unsalted butter
30 g (1 oz) plain flour
60 g (2 oz) caster sugar
2 tbsp golden syrup
CARAMELIZED PEARS
4 firm, ripe pears (preferably Comice)
500 g (1 lb 2 oz) caster sugar

500 ml (16 fl oz) water
juice of ½ lemon
TO SERVE
Vanilla Ice Cream (see page 63)
a little thin honey
few raspberries
mint leaves

1 To make the brandy snap baskets, preheat the oven to 200°C/400°F/Gas Mark 6. Mix the butter, flour and sugar together in a food processor until the texture resembles breadcrumbs. Add the golden syrup and mix to a smooth paste.

2 Divide the mixture into 4 portions. Shape each one into a ball and place well apart on 2 buttered baking sheets (two to each tray as they will spread in the oven).

3 Bake, one tray at a time, for about 7 minutes, until golden brown. Leave on the baking sheet for a few seconds, then carefully place each one over an upturned ramekin dish and mould the edges to form a tulip shape. Leave until set hard, then carefully remove. If the brandy snaps harden before you have time to shape them, return to the baking sheet and place in the oven for a few seconds to soften.

4 For the caramelized pears, put half of the sugar in a medium saucepan with the water and lemon juice. Heat gently until the sugar is dissolved, then bring to the boil.

5 Peel the pears, leaving the stalk intact. Stand them in the boiling syrup, turn down the heat to a gentle simmer and cook for 30-50 minutes, depending on ripeness, until translucent and tender. Leave to cool in the syrup.

6 Drain the pears thoroughly and lay on their side on a board. Slice each one crosswise into 7 slices, retaining the stalk in the last slice.

7 Reassemble the pears on a baking sheet fanning the slices out from top to base. Sprinkle with the remaining caster sugar and place under a preheated high grill or use a blow torch to caramelize the sugar.

8 Arrange the pear slices overlapping in sequence, in a curve on each serving plate, ending with the pear stalk. Place a brandy snap basket on each plate and add a ball of ice cream. Trickle the pears with honey and decorate with raspberries and mint to serve.

WALNUT TART

SERVES 6-8

105 g (3½ oz) plain flour
pinch of salt
55 g (1¾ oz) caster sugar
45 g (1½ oz) ground almonds
30 g (1 oz) full-fat soft cream cheese,
such as Philadelphia
80 g (2¾ oz) butter, melted
2 egg yolks

2 eggs
70 g (2¼ oz) brown sugar
60 g (2 oz) golden syrup
20 g (¾ oz) maple syrup
180 g (6 oz) shelled walnuts
3 tbsp apricot jam
grated rind and juice of ½ orange
caster sugar for sprinkling

1 Sift the flour and salt together and tip into the food processor bowl. Add the caster sugar and ground almonds, and work briefly until evenly mixed.

2 Add the cream cheese, a quarter of the butter, and the egg yolks. Process briefly to form a soft dough. Gather the dough with your hands and knead lightly until smooth. Wrap in cling film and chill in the refrigerator for 30 minutes. Meanwhile, preheat the oven to 180°C/350°F/ Gas Mark 4.

3 Roll out three quarters of the dough on a lightly floured surface to a 5 mm (¼ inch) thickness and use to line a buttered 20 cm

(8 inch) loose-bottomed flan tin (or flan ring set on a baking sheet).

4 Put the remaining butter in a blender or food processor with the whole eggs, brown sugar, golden and maple syrups, walnuts, apricot jam orange rind and juice. Process briefly until evenly mixed and the nuts are coarsely chopped. Pour into the pastry case.

5 Roll out the remaining dough to a 20 cm (8 inch) round for the lid. Brush the edges of the pastry case with water, then position the lid over the filling and press the pastry edges together to seal. Bake for 35-40 minutes until the filling is set. Sprinkle with sugar to glaze.

LEMON AND PASSION FRUIT TART

SERVES 8

FOR THE SWEET PASTRY
110 g (3¾ oz) butter, softened
30 g (1 oz) icing sugar
1 egg
140 g (4½ oz) plain flour, sifted
pinch of salt
40 g (1¼ oz) ground almonds
FOR THE FILLING
finely grated zest of 1 lemon

200 ml (7 fl oz) lemon juice
250 ml (8 fl oz) double cream
4 eggs
320 g (11 oz) caster sugar
1 passion fruit
TO GLAZE
50 g (1¾ oz) apricot jam, warmed and sieved

1 To make the pastry, cream the butter and icing sugar together in a bowl until pale and fluffy. Beat in the egg, then gradually incorporate the flour, salt and ground almonds. Work the ingredients together to form a smooth dough. Wrap in cling film and leave to rest in the refrigerator for 20 minutes. Meanwhile preheat the oven to 200°C/400°F/Gas Mark 6.

2 Roll out the pastry on a lightly floured surface to a 5 mm (¼ inch) thickness and use to line a 20 cm (8 inch) loose-bottomed flan tin which is 3 cm (1¼ inches) deep, (or flan ring placed on a baking sheet). Line with grease-proof paper and weight down with baking beans. Bake blind for 15 minutes. Remove the paper and beans. Bake for a further 5 minutes to cook the base. Allow to cool. Reduce the oven setting to 150°C/300°F/Gas Mark 2.

3 Put the lemon zest and juice in a bowl and whisk in the cream and eggs. Finally whisk in the sugar. Pass the mixture through a fine sieve, then pour into the pastry case.

4 Halve the passion fruit and squeeze the pulp and seeds on top of the lemon filling.

5 Carefully place the flan in the middle of the oven and bake for 40 minutes until set, making sure the custard does not boil. Remove from the oven and brush thinly with the apricot jam to glaze. Allow to cool before serving.

Fig and Raspberry Royale; Lemon and Passion Fruit Tart (page 91)

FIG AND RASPBERRY ROYALE

SERVES 4

10 fresh figs

16 raspberries

80 ml (5½ tbsp) port

50 g (1¾ oz) sugar

20 ml (4 tsp) Grand Marnier

450 ml (¾ pint) double cream

mint sprigs to decorate

1 Trim the tops off the figs, then slice crosswise. Reserve 12 even slices; set aside the rest of the figs for the purée.

2 Line the bases of 4 tall wine glasses with 3 fig slices and add 3 raspberries to each glass. Moisten with a teaspoonful of the port.

3 Put the remaining figs, sugar, port and Grand Marnier in a food processor or blender and work to a purée. Turn into a bowl, cover and allow to stand for 30 minutes.

4 Whip the cream in another bowl until it forms soft peaks, then lightly fold in the fig purée to create a marbled effect and carefully spoon into 4 glasses.

5 Decorate each serving with a raspberry and a mint sprig.

DAMSON COMPOTE WITH CLOTTED CREAM

SERVES 4

1 orange
50 g (1¾ oz) caster sugar
200 ml (7 fl oz) water
300 g (10 oz) ripe damsons, stoned

1 cinnamon stick
2 tbsp kirsch
2 tsp cornflour
clotted cream to serve

1 Pare the zest from the orange in long strips. Put the sugar and water in a saucepan over a low heat until the sugar is dissolved, then bring to the boil.
2 Add the damsons, orange zest, cinnamon stick and kirsch and bring to a simmer.
3 Meanwhile, mix the cornflour with a little cold water to a smooth paste. Stir into the damson compote and cook, stirring, for a few minutes until slightly thickened. Remove from the heat and allow to cool.
4 Discard the orange zest and cinnamon stick. Spoon the damson compote into serving bowls and accompany with clotted cream.

GRANNY SMITH SORBET

SERVES 4

This original, refreshing sorbet has a truly wonderful flavour. The skin of the apples imparts an attractive pale green colour.

100 g (3½ oz) caster sugar
150 ml (¼ pint) water
5 tsp lemon juice

500 g (1 lb 2 oz) Granny Smith apples
apple mint sprigs to decorate

1 Put the sugar, water and lemon juice in a small pan and dissolve over a low heat, then bring to the boil. Remove from the heat and leave to cool.
2 Quarter and core the apples, but do not peel. Work to a purée, using a hand blender or food processor. Pass through a sieve into a bowl. Stir in the sugar syrup.
3 Freeze in an ice-cream maker according to the manufacturer's instructions. Alternatively pour the mixture into a freezerproof container, cover and freeze until almost firm. Transfer to a food processor and whizz to break down the ice crystals. Return to the container and freeze again. Repeat this process twice more to ensure a smooth, fine-textured result.
4 To serve, scoop into glass dishes and decorate with mint sprigs.

OPERA CHOCOLATE SLICE

SERVES 8-10

FOR THE SPONGE

6 eggs, separated

160 g (5½ oz) icing sugar

90 g (3 oz) plain flour, sifted

90 g (3 oz) ground almonds

TO ASSEMBLE

2 tsp instant coffee

300 ml (½ pint) water

100 g (3½ oz) butter

100 g (3½ oz) Fondant (see page 24)

130 g (4½ oz) chocolate

2 tbsp double cream

300 g (10 oz) caster sugar

2 tbsp rum

cocoa powder for dusting

1 Preheat oven to 200°C/400°F/Gas Mark 6. Draw three 25 cm (10 inch) squares on sheets of non-stick baking parchment and invert onto baking sheets.

2 For the sponge, whisk the egg whites in a bowl until they form stiff peaks. Gradually whisk in the icing sugar to make a smooth stiff meringue.

3 Very quickly, incorporate the egg yolks, so that the meringue turns yellow; do not over-mix. Carefully fold in the flour and ground almonds.

4 Divide the mixture into 3 equal portions. Spread each portion on a prepared baking sheet to a 25 cm (10 inch) square, approximately 5 mm (¼ inch) thick.

5 Bake in the oven for 8-10 minutes until golden in colour. Slide the sponge and paper off the baking sheets and allow to cool.

6 To make the butter cream, dissolve 1 tsp of the coffee in 2 tsp of the hot water. Beat the butter and fondant together in a bowl until light and fluffy, then beat in the dissolved coffee. Divide this mixture into 2 equal portions.

7 For the chocolate cream, break 70 g (2½ oz) chocolate into small pieces. Bring the cream to the boil in a pan, then remove from the heat and stir in the chocolate. Allow to cool.

8 For the coffee punch, put the remaining coffee and water in a saucepan with the caster sugar and rum. Bring to the boil, stirring to dissolve the sugar and coffee. Remove from the heat and allow to cool until lukewarm.

9 To assemble the layered slice, melt the remaining 60 g (2 oz) chocolate in a bowl over a pan of hot water, stirring until smooth. Spread evenly over one of the sponge squares and allow to set. Place chocolate-side down on a sheet of non-stick baking parchment.

10 Sprinkle a third of the coffee punch over this base sponge. Spread evenly with half of the butter cream, then position another sponge on top. Saturate this sponge with half the remaining coffee punch. Spread with the chocolate cream.

11 Cover with the final sponge and saturate with the remaining coffee punch. Spread evenly with the rest of the butter cream and refrigerate for 1 hour.

12 To serve, dust with cocoa powder and cut into slices using a warm knife.

CHOCOLATE GÂTEAU WITH GRAND MARNIER

SERVES 6

70 g (2¼ oz) plain flour
30 g (1 oz) caster sugar
40 g (1¼ oz) unsalted butter (at room temperature)
1 egg yolk
1 Genoese Sponge Cake (see page 60)
2 tbsp orange marmalade, warmed and sieved

125 ml (4 fl oz) orange juice
5 tbsp Grand Marnier
2 gelatine leaves
350 g (12 oz) milk chocolate, in pieces
300 ml (½ pint) double cream
2 tbsp coarsely ground walnuts

1 To make the shortbread base, mix the flour and sugar together in a bowl, then rub in the butter until the mixture resembles fine crumbs. Add the egg yolk and bind to a smooth dough.
2 Transfer to a baking sheet lined with non-stick baking parchment and press out to a neat round 5 mm (¼ inch) thick and 17.5 cm (7 inches) in diameter. Prick the surface all over with a fork. Chill in the refrigerator for 15 minutes. Meanwhile, preheat the oven to 180°C/350°F/Gas Mark 4.
3 Bake the shortbread for 12 minutes or until golden. Leave on the baking sheet for a few minutes then transfer to a wire rack to cool.
4 Cut a 5 mm (¼ inch) layer from the sponge cake and trim to the same size as the shortbread. (Use the rest for another recipe.)
5 Line the side of an 18.5 cm (7½ inch) spring-form cake tin with non-stick baking parchment. Place the cooled shortbread in the tin and spread evenly with the marmalade. Position the sponge cake layer on top and press gently.
6 Using a pastry brush, moisten the cake with half of the orange juice and 1½ tbsp of the Grand Marnier.
7 For the mousse, soak the gelatine leaves in cold water for 10 minutes until softened.
8 Drain the gelatine leaves and squeeze out excess water, then return to the bowl and add the remaining orange juice and Grand Marnier. Set the bowl in a pan of simmering water and stir until the gelatine is melted; do not boil.
9 Melt the chocolate in a heatproof bowl over a pan of simmering water; cool slightly.
10 Whip the cream in another bowl until soft peaks form. Stir the gelatine mixture into the melted chocolate, then fold in the cream to give a smooth velvety consistency.
11 Pour the chocolate mixture slowly around the edge of the cake, to fill the gap between the cake and the flan ring, then pour the rest on top of the cake and smooth the surface.
12 Sprinkle with the walnuts, then cover and chill in the refrigerator for about 1½ hours or until the mousse is set.
13 Carefully unmould the gâteau to serve.

Winter

Mince Pies

Mrs Wood's Christmas Pudding
with Brandy Sauce

Sticky Toffee Pudding

Romilly's Chocolate Kugelhupf

Queen of Puddings

Mincemeat Soufflé

Apple wrapped in Puff Pastry with
a Calvados Butter Sauce

Dried Fruit Tart with Streusel

Exotic Fruit Tartlets

Apricot and Almond Tartlets

Pecan Pie

Coffee and Praline Pot Crème

Banana Brulée

Linzertorte

Pear and Ginger Strudel

Spiced Wine with Fruit and Ice Cream

Chocolate Sunrise Parfait

Carrot and Clementine Ice Cream

Coconut and Pineapple Ice Cream

Yule Log

Rich Chocolate Gâteau

Stollen

MINCE PIES

MAKES 25

140 g (4½ oz) butter
15 g (½ oz) lard
100 g (3½ oz) icing sugar
1 egg
250 g (8½ oz) plain flour

35 g (1¼ oz) ground almonds
½ quantity mincemeat (see below)
1 egg white, beaten, to glaze
caster sugar for sprinkling

1 Cream the butter, lard and icing sugar together in a bowl until very pale, then beat in the egg a little at a time.
2 Mix in the flour and ground almonds and knead to a smooth dough; take care to avoid overmixing. Wrap in cling film and leave to rest in the refrigerator for 1 hour. Preheat the oven to 180°C/350°F/Gas Mark 4.
3 Roll out the pastry on a lightly floured surface to a 3 mm (⅛ inch) thickness. Cut out 25 rounds 7 cm (2¾ inches) in diameter, and 25 rounds 6 cm (2½ inches) in diameter.
4 Line 25 lightly oiled tartlet moulds with the larger pastry rounds. Fill with mincemeat and top with the smaller rounds, sealing the edges.
5 Brush with egg white and sprinkle with sugar. Bake in the oven for 20-25 minutes. Remove from the tartlet tins and serve warm.

MINCEMEAT

100 g (3½ oz) dried figs
100 g (3½ oz) dried apricots
400 g (14 oz) raisins
100 g (3½ oz) sultanas
100 g (3½ oz) candied mixed peel
2 tbsp orange marmalade
2 tbsp black treacle
4 Cox's apples

300 g (10 oz) shredded suet
240 g (8 oz) soft brown sugar
1 tsp freshly grated nutmeg
½ tsp ground cinnamon
½ tsp ground ginger
finely grated zest of 1 lemon
150 ml (¼ pint) brandy

1 Put the dried fruit, peel, marmalade and treacle in a food processor and process briefly until roughly chopped. Transfer to a mixing bowl.
2 Peel, core and grate the apples; stir into the mixture. Add the suet, sugar, spices, lemon zest and brandy. Stir gently to mix, then cover and set aside in a cool place for 24 hours.
3 Stir well and spoon into sterilized jars or an airtight container. Store in a cool, dry place. Makes about 1.4 kg (3 lb)

MRS WOOD'S CHRISTMAS PUDDING

SERVES 8

120 g (4 oz) shredded suet
60 g (2 oz) self-raising flour
120 g (4 oz) fresh white breadcrumbs
1 tsp ground mixed spice
1/4 tsp freshly grated nutmeg
large pinch of ground cinnamon
240 g (8 oz) dark brown soft sugar
540 g (1 lb 3 oz) luxury mixed dried
fruit (raisins, sultanas, currants, etc)
30 g (1 oz) mixed candied peel, chopped
30 g (1 oz) blanched almonds, chopped
finely grated zest of 1/2 large orange

1 small cooking apple, peeled, cored and
finely chopped
finely grated zest of 1/2 large lemon
150 ml (1/4 pint) stout, such as Guinness
70 ml (4 1/2 tbsp) rum or brandy
2 small eggs (size 4 or 5)

BRANDY SAUCE
45 g (1 1/2 oz) cornflour
500 ml (16 fl oz) milk
100 g (3 1/2 oz) caster sugar
2 tbsp brandy

1 Put the suet, flour, breadcrumbs, spices and sugar into a large mixing bowl and mix thoroughly. Gradually stir in the dried fruit, candied peel and almonds, followed by the grated citrus zests and apple.

2 Pour the stout and rum or brandy into a small bowl, add the eggs and beat thoroughly. Stir into the fruit mixture; it should have a fairly sloppy consistency.

3 Cover and leave in a cool place overnight.

4 The next day, spoon the mixture into a lightly greased 1.2 litre (2 pint) pudding basin. Cover with a double thickness of greaseproof paper, pleating it in the middle (to allow for expansion during cooking). Cover this with a pleated sheet of foil and secure with string.

5 Place the pudding in a large saucepan on an upturned saucer. Pour in enough boiling water to come halfway up the side of the basin. Cover tightly and cook for 7-8 hours, checking the water level from time to time and replenishing with boiling water as necessary.

6 Allow to cool completely. When the pudding is cold, replace the greaseproof paper and foil covers with fresh ones. Store in a cool place until required.

7 On the day, steam the pudding as before for 2 hours.

8 Meanwhile make the brandy sauce. Mix the cornflour with 2 tbsp of the milk until smooth. Put the remaining milk in a saucepan with the sugar and bring to the boil, stirring to dissolve the sugar. Whisk in the cornflour and simmer, stirring, for 2 minutes until thickened and smooth. Remove from the heat and stir in the brandy. Pass through a sieve into a serving jug.

9 To serve, turn out the pudding onto a warmed plate. Serve with the brandy sauce.

Sticky Toffee Pudding

STICKY TOFFEE PUDDING

SERVES 8

This irresistible rich pudding is worth every calorie!

135 ml (4½ fl oz) double cream
180 g (6 oz) butter
60 g (2 oz) dark muscovado sugar
150 g (5 oz) soft brown sugar
4 eggs, separated

180 g (6 oz) plain flour
1 tbsp baking powder
90 g (3 oz) stoned dates, chopped
1 tsp finely grated lemon zest
1 tsp finely grated orange zest

1 Put the cream and half of the butter in a small saucepan over a moderate heat until the butter is melted and the mixture comes to the boil. Add the muscovado sugar, stirring until dissolved. Pour half of the sauce into the base of a greased 1.2 litre (2 pint) pudding basin; set aside the rest of the sauce for serving.
2 Cream the remaining butter and soft brown sugar together in a bowl until light and fluffy. Beat in the egg yolks, one at a time.
3 Sift the flour and baking powder together and stir into the mixture until evenly incorporated; the pudding mix will have a thick consistency.
4 Fold in the chopped dates and leave to rest for 5-10 minutes.
5 In the meantime, whisk the egg whites in a separate bowl until they form soft peaks. Whisk in the grated lemon and orange zests. Gradually fold into the pudding mixture, a third at a time.

6 Spoon the mixture into the prepared pudding basin. Cover with a circle of non-stick baking parchment. Cover the basin with foil and secure with string.
7 Stand the pudding in a large saucepan and pour in enough boiling water to come halfway up the sides of the basin. Cover and steam the pudding for 2 hours, topping up with boiling water as necessary.
8 To serve, remove the foil and paper. Turn out the pudding onto a warmed serving dish and pour the remaining toffee sauce over the pudding before serving.

NOTE: You can make individual puddings if preferred. Use 150 ml (¼ pint) individual pudding basins. Cook in a bain-marie, covered with foil, in the oven at 180°C/350°F/Gas Mark 4 for 40-50 minutes.

ROMILLY'S CHOCOLATE KUGELHUPF

SERVES 4

260 g (9 oz) dark chocolate
100 g (3½ oz) unsalted butter
40 g (1¼ oz) icing sugar
4 eggs, separated

40 g (1¼ oz) plain flour, sifted
icing sugar for dusting
Vanilla Ice Cream (see page 63) to serve

1 Preheat oven to 180°C/350°F/Gas Mark 4. Butter 4 ovenproof tea cups.
2 Melt 200 g (7 oz) of the dark chocolate in a heatproof bowl over a pan of simmering water, stirring until smooth.
3 Cream the butter and icing sugar together in a bowl until light and fluffy. Gradually beat in the egg yolks, then fold in the melted chocolate. Fold in the flour until evenly incorporated.
4 Whisk the egg whites in a separate bowl until they form soft peaks, then carefully fold into the warm chocolate mixture.
5 Half-fill the cups with the mixture. Break the remaining chocolate into 4 pieces and put one piece in the centre of each cup. Top up with the mixture to three-quarters fill the cups.
6 Bake in the oven for 12-14 minutes until risen and just firm to the touch.
7 Turn out immediately onto serving plates and dust with icing sugar. Serve with ice cream.

QUEEN OF PUDDINGS

SERVES 4

250 ml (8 fl oz) milk
250 ml (8 fl oz) cream
150 g (5 oz) caster sugar
finely grated zest of 1 lemon
60 g (2 oz) butter

125 g (4¼ oz) fresh white breadcrumbs
2 egg yolks
50 g (1¾ oz) apricot jam, warmed and sieved
4 egg whites

1 Preheat oven to 150°C/300°F/Gas Mark 2. Pour the milk and cream into a saucepan and slowly bring to the boil. Add 50 g (1¾ oz) of the sugar, the lemon zest and butter.
2 Remove from the heat and stir in the breadcrumbs, then beat in the egg yolks.

3 Grease a 900 ml (1½ pint) shallow pie dish and place in a bain-marie (or roasting tin containing enough warm water to come halfway up the sides). Pour the milk mixture into the pie dish and bake in the oven for 25-30 minutes until set.

4 Gently brush the apricot jam over the top, taking care to avoid breaking the skin.

5 Warm the remaining sugar in the oven for 5-10 minutes. Meanwhile, whisk the egg whites in a bowl until they form stiff peaks. Gradually whisk in the warmed sugar to form a stiff, glossy meringue.

6 Using a piping bag fitted with a fluted nozzle, pipe a meringue lattice on top of the pudding. Place under a preheated hot grill until golden (or use a blow torch to colour the meringue).

7 Serve warm or cold, with cream.

MINCEMEAT SOUFFLÉ

SERVES 4

250 ml (8 fl oz) milk	90 g (3 oz) sugar
40 g (1¼ oz) plain flour	100 g (3½ oz) mincemeat
40 g (1¼ oz) butter	6 egg whites
5 egg yolks	2 tsp cornflour

1 Generously butter 4 individual soufflé dishes, about 10 cm (4 inches) in diameter, then sprinkle with sugar. Preheat the oven to 220°C/425°F/Gas Mark 7.

2 Bring the milk to the boil in a saucepan. Meanwhile mix the flour and butter to a paste to form a beurre manié. Add the beurre manié to the hot milk, a small piece at a time, whisking all the time. Bring back to the boil and cook, stirring, until thickened and smooth. Remove from the heat.

3 Beat in the egg yolks, one at a time. Stir in half of the sugar and the mincemeat. Let cool.

4 In another large clean bowl, whisk the egg whites until stiff, then whisk in the remaining sugar together with the cornflour, until the meringue forms firm peaks. Stir a spoonful of the meringue into the mincemeat mixture to loosen it, then gently fold in the rest of the meringue.

5 Divide the mixture between the prepared soufflé dishes. Stand the dishes in a bain-marie (or roasting tin containing enough hot water to come halfway up the sides of the dishes). Bake in the oven for about 15-20 minutes until well risen and golden. Serve immediately.

APPLE WRAPPED IN PUFF PASTRY WITH A CALVADOS BUTTER SAUCE

SERVES 4

This is probably my all-time favourite winter pudding. The Calvados butter sauce and apple work together like a dream.

75 g (2½ oz) sultanas

25 ml (1½ tbsp) Calvados

ground cinnamon for sprinkling

4 dessert apples, preferably Reinette

300 g (10 oz) puff pastry

1 egg yolk, beaten

50 g (1½ oz) caster sugar

50 ml (3 tbsp) water

1 tbsp liquid glucose

50 g (1¾ oz) unsalted butter

150 ml (¼ pint) double cream

25 g (¾ oz) icing sugar

1 Put the sultanas in a small bowl, pour on the Calvados and leave to soak for at least 1 hour.

2 Preheat oven to 190°C/375°F/Gas Mark 5. Drain the sultanas, reserving the Calvados, and sprinkle with a little cinnamon. Peel the apples, remove the cores and cut a slice from the base of each one so they stand level. Fill the centre of each apple with sultanas.

3 Roll out the puff pastry on a lightly floured surface to a 3 mm (⅛ inch) thickness. Cut out 4 ovals, each about 18 x 12 cm (7 x 5 inches) and brush the edges with beaten egg yolk.

4 Place an apple in the middle of each pastry oval and bring the pastry edges up over the top to completely enclose the fruit. Seal the edges well and crimp with a small knife. Brush the pastry with beaten egg yolk and make a small slit in the top of each parcel. Bake for about 20 minutes.

5 Meanwhile, make the sauce. Put the caster sugar, water and glucose in a heavy-based saucepan over a low heat until the sugar is dissolved, then increase the heat and cook to a pale amber-coloured caramel. Carefully stir in the butter and all but 25 ml (1½ tbsp) of the cream, then add the reserved Calvados. Pass through a fine sieve into a bowl.

6 Dust the apple parcels generously with icing sugar and place under a preheated grill to glaze. Position each one on a warmed plate and surround with the sauce. Feather the sauce with the reserved cream. Serve at once.

Apple wrapped in Puff Pastry with a Calvados Butter Sauce

DRIED FRUIT TART WITH STREUSEL

SERVES 8

The amaretto gives this tart a tremendous lift. Serve it warm or cold, with a little double cream.

250 g (8½ oz) Sweet Pastry (see page 15)
75 g (2½ oz) dried apricots, diced
75 g (2½ oz) stoned prunes, diced
75 g (2½ oz) dried figs, diced
75 g (2½ oz) sultanas
3 tbsp amaretto liqueur
5 tbsp water

FOR THE CUSTARD LAYER
2 egg yolks

45 g (1½ oz) caster sugar
100 ml (3½ fl oz) double cream
½ vanilla pod

FOR THE STREUSEL
60 g (2 oz) plain flour
50 g (1¾ oz) caster sugar
30 g (1 oz) ground almonds
1 tsp ground allspice
50 g (1¾ oz) unsalted butter

1 Roll out the pastry on a lightly floured surface to about a 3 mm (⅛ inch) thickness and use to line a deep 20 cm (8 inch) flan tin. Line the pastry case with greaseproof paper or foil and weigh it down with baking beans. Leave to rest in the refrigerator for 15 minutes. Meanwhile preheat the oven to 190°C/375°F/ Gas Mark 5.

2 Bake the pastry case for 15 minutes, then remove the paper and beans and bake for a further 5 minutes, until golden brown.

3 Meanwhile, put the dried fruit, liqueur and water in a pan. Bring to a simmer and simmer gently for 5 minutes. Leave to cool, by which time the fruit will have absorbed the liquid.

4 When the pastry case is cooked, remove from

the oven and reduce the setting to 180°C/350°F/ Gas Mark 4.

5 For the custard layer, put the egg yolks, sugar and cream in a bowl. Scrape the seeds from the vanilla pod into the bowl and mix well until smooth.

6 Spread the dried fruit over the base of the pastry case and pour the custard on top. Bake for 15 minutes.

7 For the streusel, put all of the ingredients in a food processor and process briefly; or mix the dry ingredients together in a bowl and rub in the butter by hand, until the mixture resembles breadcrumbs. Sprinkle the streusel over the tart and return to the oven for 15 minutes, until the topping is crisp. Serve warm or cold.

EXOTIC FRUIT TARTLETS

SERVES 4

100 g (3½ oz) puff pastry
½ quantity Frangipane (see page 87)
1 tbsp sieved passion fruit juice
4 tbsp pastry cream (see page 84), or whipped cream
½ kiwi fruit, peeled and sliced
¼ mango, peeled, stoned and sliced

¼ small pineapple, peeled, cored and sliced
¼ pawpaw, peeled, deseeded and sliced
TO GLAZE
4 tbsp apricot jam, warmed and sieved
TO DECORATE
4 tiny mint sprigs

1 Roll out the puff pastry on a lightly floured surface and use to line four 7.5 cm (3 inch) tartlet tins. Leave to rest in the refrigerator for 15 minutes. Meanwhile, preheat the oven to 200°C/400°F/Gas Mark 6.
2 Divide the frangipane between the pastry cases and bake in the oven for 10–15 minutes until golden brown. Leave to cool.
3 Stir the passion fruit juice into the pastry cream or whipped cream, then spoon the cream into the tartlets.
4 Arrange the exotic fruit decoratively on top. Brush with apricot jam to glaze and decorate with mint sprigs.

APRICOT AND ALMOND TARTLETS

SERVES 4

450 ml (¾ pint) Sugar Syrup (see page 86)

8 fresh apricots, halved and stoned

240 g (8 oz) Sweet Pastry (see page 15)

200 g (7 oz) Frangipane (see page 87 – double quantity)

icing sugar for dusting

25 g (¾ oz) pistachio nuts, finely chopped

Coconut and Pineapple Ice Cream (see page 122) to serve

1 Heat the sugar syrup in a saucepan, add the apricot halves and poach until just tender. Drain thoroughly and leave to cool.

2 Roll out the pastry to a 3 mm (⅛ inch) thickness and use to line 4 deep 8 cm (3¼ inch) tartlet tins. Chill in the refrigerator for 20 minutes. Meanwhile, preheat the oven to 180°C/350°F/Gas Mark 4.

3 Dice the poached apricot halves and divide between the pastry cases. Cover with the frangipane and spread evenly. Bake for about 20 minutes until the frangipane is golden. Allow to cool until warm.

4 Dust with icing sugar and decorate with chopped pistachio nuts. Serve with coconut and pineapple ice cream.

  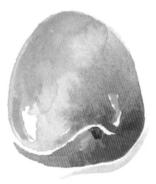

Apricot and Almond Tartlets; Pecan Pie (page 112)

PECAN PIE

SERVES 6-8

250 g (8½ oz) Sweet Pastry (see page 15)
180 g (6 oz) pecan nuts
2 eggs (size 3)
125 g (4 oz) brown sugar
60 g (2 oz) butter, melted

30 g (1 oz) maple syrup
75 g (2½ oz) golden syrup
2-3 tbsp apricot jam, warmed and sieved, to glaze

1 Roll out the sweet pastry dough thinly on a lightly floured surface and use to line a buttered deep 20 cm (8 inch) loose-bottomed flan tin (or flan ring set on a baking sheet). Prick the base with a fork. Line with greaseproof paper and weight down with baking beans. Leave to rest in a cool place for 20 minutes, while you preheat the oven to 200°C/400°F/Gas Mark 6.
2 Bake blind for 12 minutes, then remove the beans and paper and bake for a further 5 minutes, until golden brown. Allow to cool. Lower the oven setting to 180°C/350°F/Gas Mark 4.

3 Set aside a quarter of the pecan nuts. Place the rest in a blender or food processor with the eggs, sugar, melted butter, maple and golden syrups. Work until evenly mixed and the nuts are coarsely chopped. Pour into the pastry case.
4 Arrange the whole pecan nuts on top in a circular pattern, pressing them in lightly. Bake in the oven for about 30-35 minutes until the filling is set.
5 Lightly brush the surface with the warm apricot jam to glaze. Serve warm or cold, with whipped cream.

COFFEE AND PRALINE POT CRÈME

SERVES 4

400 ml (14 fl oz) milk

1 tsp instant coffee powder

100 ml (3½ fl oz) double cream

1 egg

3 egg yolks

100 g (3½ oz) sugar

TO DECORATE

whipped cream

1 tbsp Praline Croquant (see below)

1 Preheat oven to 150°C/300°F/Gas Mark 2. Heat 100 ml (3½ fl oz) of the milk in a saucepan to a simmer. Pour onto the coffee, stirring to dissolve. Add the rest of the milk and the cream; heat to just below simmering.

2 Beat the whole egg, egg yolks and sugar together in a bowl until pale. Pour on the coffee milk mixture, stirring all the time.

3 Pass through a fine sieve into a jug and skim off any froth from the surface with a spoon.

4 Divide between 4 custard pots or ramekins.

5 Stand them in a bain-marie (or roasting tin containing sufficient water to come 1 cm (½ inch) below the rims of the dishes). Cover the tin with foil and cook in the oven for 25–30 minutes; do not allow the water to boil. The crèmes are ready when the surface feels tight when lightly pressed.

6 Remove the dishes from the bain-marie and allow to cool.

7 Top each crème with a spoonful of cream and a sprinkling of praline croquant.

PRALINE CROQUANT

150 g (5 oz) flaked almonds

200 g (7 oz) sugar

juice of ½ lemon

1 Preheat oven to 180°C/350°F/Gas Mark 4. Spread the almonds out on a baking tray and toast in the oven for 8-10 minutes until golden.

2 Meanwhile, melt half the sugar in a small heavy-based pan over a low heat. Carefully add the lemon juice and cook, stirring continuously, until the sugar turns to a light caramel.

3 Add the remaining sugar a little at a time, keeping the caramel an amber colour. Mix in the warm almonds.

4 Pour the praline onto a baking sheet lined with non-stick baking parchment and leave until cold and set hard. Break into pieces, then crush with a rolling pin and use as required.

BANANA BRÛLÉE

SERVES 4

3 egg yolks
200 ml (7 fl oz) double cream
60 ml (2 fl oz) banana milk shake
flavouring

90 g (3 oz) caster sugar
4 bananas

1 Preheat oven to 150°C/300°F/Gas Mark 2. In a bowl, whisk the egg yolks with the cream, banana milk shake flavouring and 50 g (1¾ oz) of the sugar until pale and creamy. Pass through a fine sieve into a clean bowl.
2 Cut 1 banana into slices and divide between 4 ramekins. Pour the cream mixture on top.
3 Stand the ramekins in a bain-marie (or roasting tin containing enough warm water to come halfway up the sides of the ramekins). Cook in the oven for 30 minutes or until set. Remove from the oven and allow to cool.
4 Slice the remaining bananas on the diagonal. Arrange the banana slices on top of the brûlées, overlapping them slightly. Sprinkle generously with the remaining sugar and caramelize under a preheated high grill (or use a blow torch). Serve at once.

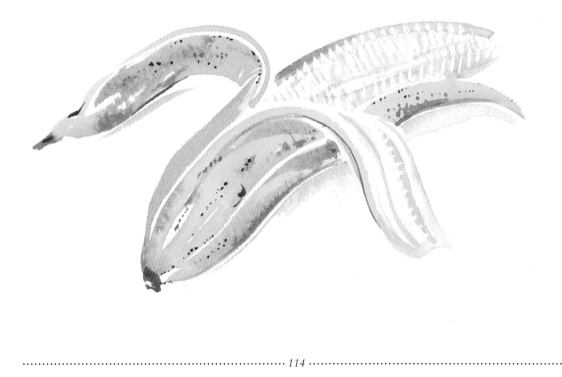

LINZERTORTE

SERVES 8

150 g (5 oz) unsalted butter

200 g (7 oz) icing sugar

1 egg, beaten

3 egg yolks

finely grated zest of 1 lemon

140 g (4½ oz) plain flour, sifted

110 g (3¾ oz) ground almonds

220 g (7¾ oz) redcurrant jelly

beaten egg to glaze

icing sugar for dusting

1 Preheat oven to 185°C/360°F/Gas Mark 4½. Cream the butter and icing sugar together in a bowl until light and fluffy. Gradually beat in the whole egg and egg yolks.

2 Stir in the lemon zest, flour and ground almonds. Knead lightly to form a smooth dough. Wrap in cling film and chill in the refrigerator for 20 minutes.

3 Roll out half of the dough on a lightly floured surface to a 5 mm (¼ inch) thickness and use to line a greased 20 cm (8 inch) loose-bottomed flan tin (or flan ring placed on a baking sheet).

4 Roll out the remaining dough to a 3 mm thickness and cut 5 mm (¼ inch) wide strips.

5 Spread the redcurrant jelly over the base of the flan case. Arrange the strips over the top to form a lattice. Brush the dough with beaten egg and bake in the oven for about 40 minutes or until the pastry is golden. Allow to cool slightly before removing from the flan tin.

6 Serve warm or cold, dusted with icing sugar.

Linzertorte (page 115); Pear and Ginger Strudel

PEAR AND GINGER STRUDEL

SERVES 6-8

4 pears
juice of ½ lemon
1 tsp ground ginger
4 sheets of filo pastry

120 g (4 oz) unsalted butter, melted
4 tbsp fresh white breadcrumbs
3 tbsp caster sugar
icing sugar for dusting

1 Preheat oven to 200°C/400°F/Gas Mark 6. Peel, core and slice the pears crosswise, then immediately toss in the lemon juice to prevent discolouration and sprinkle with the ginger.
2 Lay two sheets of filo pastry, side by side, on a large sheet of non-stick baking parchment overlapping them slightly. Brush generously with melted butter.
3 Place the other 2 sheets of filo on top and brush with more butter.
4 Sprinkle the breadcrumbs and sugar evenly over three quarters of the pastry, leaving a 2 cm (¾ inch) clear margin on the two sides, and the quarter furthest away from you free of breadcrumbs. Distribute the pear slices evenly on top of the breadcrumbs.
5 Fold both sides of the filo pastry inwards by 2 cm (¾ inch), then roll up the strudel with the help of the baking parchment, starting with the edge closest to you. Brush liberally with the rest of the melted butter and carefully lift onto a baking tray.
6 Bake in the oven for 15 minutes until the pastry is crisp and golden brown.
7 Dust liberally with icing sugar and cut into slices to serve.

SPICED WINE WITH FRUIT AND ICE CREAM

SERVES 4

400 ml (14 fl oz) red wine

2 tbsp rum

75 g (2½ oz) caster sugar

1 large orange

4 cloves

½ cinnamon stick

1 apple, peeled, cored and sliced

1 pear, peeled, cored and sliced

1 small pineapple, peeled, cored and cut into small slices

90 g (3 oz) grapes

90 g (3 oz) cherries, stoned

TO SERVE

Vanilla Ice Cream (see page 63), or other ice cream of your choice

mint sprigs to decorate

1 Put the wine, rum and sugar in a large saucepan and heat gently until the sugar is dissolved. Meanwhile, peel and segment the orange removing all white pith and pips, set aside; reserve half of the peel.

2 Add the cloves, cinnamon and reserved orange peel to the wine syrup. Bring almost to boiling point, then remove from the heat and leave to infuse for about 15 minutes.

3 Remove the spices and orange peel, then add all of the fruit to the wine and leave to warm through for a few minutes.

4 Ladle the fruit and spiced wine into warm soup bowls and top each serving with a scoop of ice cream. Decorate with mint sprigs and serve immediately.

CHOCOLATE SUNRISE PARFAIT

SERVES 4

300 ml (½ pint) double cream
200 g (7 oz) dark chocolate, in small
pieces
2 egg yolks
30 g (1 oz) caster sugar
4 Shortbread discs, each 8 cm
(3¼ inches) (see page 53)
4 small balls of Carrot and Clementine
Ice Cream (see page 120)

ORANGE SAUCE
juice of 3 oranges
2 tsp cornflour
a little sugar (optional)
2 tsp Grand Marnier
TO DECORATE
cocoa powder for dusting

1 Put 100 ml (3½ fl oz) of the cream in a small saucepan and heat until barely simmering. Remove from the heat, add the chocolate and stir until melted. Allow to cool until lukewarm.
2 Meanwhile beat the egg yolks and sugar together in a bowl until creamy, then fold in the chocolate mixture.
3 Whip the remaining cream in a separate bowl until it forms soft peaks, then fold into the mousse to give a soft, velvety texture.
4 Place a shortbread disc in each of 4 ramekins, 8 cm (3¼ inches) in diameter. Spoon on a 5 mm (¼ inch) layer of the chocolate mixture. Place one sorbet ball in the centre and quickly fill the ramekins with the remaining chocolate mixture. Level off the surface.

5 Place in the freezer for at least 4 hours until very firm.
6 To make the orange sauce, mix 1 tbsp of the orange juice with the cornflour. Bring the remaining orange juice to the boil in a saucepan. Stir in the cornflour mixture and cook stirring, for 1-2 minutes until slightly thickened. Sweeten with a little sugar if necessary. Remove from the heat and stir in the Grand Marnier. Allow to cool.
7 When ready to serve, loosen the edge of each parfait with a warm knife, then carefully unmould and place on individual serving plates.
8 Dust with a little cocoa powder and surround each chocolate parfait with a pool of orange sauce. Serve at once.

CARROT AND CLEMENTINE ICE CREAM

SERVES 4

250 ml (8 fl oz) carrot juice
50 g (1¾ oz) peeled carrots, finely grated
grated zest and juice of 3 clementines

4 egg yolks
75 g (2½ oz) caster sugar
300 ml (½ pint) double cream

1 Bring the carrot juice to the boil in a saucepan. Add the grated carrots and clementine zest and simmer for 5 minutes.
2 Allow to cool, then pass through a fine sieve into a bowl. Stir in the clementine juice.
3 Beat the egg yolks and sugar together in another bowl until pale. Meanwhile, bring the cream to the boil in a heavy-based saucepan.
4 Pour the cream onto the egg mixture, whisking until well blended.
5 Return to the pan and cook over a very low heat, stirring continuously with a wooden spoon, until the custard thickens slightly – just enough to thinly coat the back of the wooden

spoon; do not allow to boil or it will curdle.
6 Remove from the heat and add the orange and carrot mixture. Pass through a fine sieve into a chilled bowl. Allow to cool.
7 Freeze in an ice-cream machine according to the manufacturer's instructions. Alternatively, pour the mixture into a large freezerproof bowl, cover and freeze until almost set. Transfer to a food processor and whisk to break down the ice crystals. Put the mixture back into the bowl, cover and return to the freezer. Repeat this process twice, then freeze until firm.
8 Scoop the ice cream into balls and serve in glass dishes.

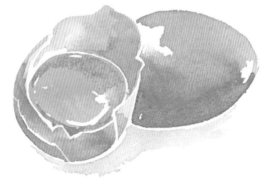

Carrot and Clementine Ice Cream; Coconut and Pineapple Ice Cream (page 122)

COCONUT AND PINEAPPLE ICE CREAM

SERVES 6

1 medium pineapple

6 egg yolks

150 g (5 oz) caster sugar

500 ml (16 fl oz) milk

250 ml (8 fl oz) double cream

75 ml (5 tbsp) canned cream of coconut

mint sprigs to decorate

1 Peel, halve and core the pineapple. Roughly chop the pineapple flesh and place in a blender or food processor. Work until smooth then transfer to a bowl and set aside.

2 Beat the egg yolks and sugar together in a bowl until pale.

3 Meanwhile, put the milk, cream and cream of coconut into a heavy-based saucepan and bring to the boil. Pour onto the egg mixture, whisking all the time.

4 Return to the pan and cook over a very low heat, stirring continuously, until the custard thickens slightly – just enough to coat the back of a wooden spoon.

5 Remove from the heat and stir in the puréed pineapple. Pass through a fine sieve into a chilled bowl and cool quickly over a bowl of iced water, stirring occasionally.

6 Freeze in an ice-cream machine according to the manufacturer's instructions. Alternatively, pour the mixture into a large freezerproof bowl, cover and place in the freezer until frozen around the edge. Whisk vigorously or use a hand-held blender to break down the ice crystals. Cover and return to the freezer. Repeat this process twice, then freeze until firm.

7 Scoop the ice cream into balls and serve in glass dishes, decorated with mint sprigs.

YULE LOG

SERVES 6

3 eggs (size 3)
100 g (3½ oz) sugar
125 g (4¼ oz) plain flour
35 g (1¼ oz) cocoa powder

2 tbsp warm water
1 quantity Chocolate Butter Cream (see below)
icing sugar for dusting

1 Preheat oven to 220°C/425°F/Gas Mark 7. Whisk the eggs and sugar together in a bowl until pale and thick. Sift the flour and cocoa powder together and carefully fold into the egg mixture, then fold in the water.
2 Spread the mixture evenly to a 30 cm (12 inch) square on a large baking sheet lined with greaseproof paper. Bake for 12 minutes.
3 Spread the warm sponge thinly with

chocolate butter cream. Trim off the edges and roll up the sponge to form a log.
4 Spread the remaining buttercream over the log, then draw a comb scraper or fork over the surface to represent the bark of a tree. Cut a 10 cm (4 inch) wedge off the roll at an angle, for a branch and position to one side, attaching the cut-side to the roll with a little butter cream. Dust with icing sugar to serve.

CHOCOLATE BUTTER CREAM

120 g (4 oz) caster sugar
4 tbsp water
pinch of cream of tartar

4 egg yolks, beaten
300 g (10 oz) butter
80 g (2¾ oz) plain chocolate

1 Put the sugar, water and cream of tartar in a small heavy-based pan and heat slowly until the sugar is dissolved.
2 Increase the heat and boil until the syrup registers 115°C/240°F on a sugar thermometer; ie the soft ball stage is reached. Immediately pour the syrup onto the beaten egg yolks, whisking all the time. Continue whisking until the mixture is cool.

3 Cream the butter in a bowl, then gradually beat into the cooled egg and syrup mixture.
4 Melt the chocolate in a heatproof bowl over a pan of hot water, then beat into the butter cream.

NOTE: This quantity is sufficient for the Yule Log (above), or for filling and topping a 20 cm (8 inch) gâteau.

RICH CHOCOLATE GÂTEAU

SERVES 10

FOR THE SPONGE

220 g (7¾ oz) butter

190 g (6½ oz) caster sugar

10 eggs, separated

120 g (4 oz) plain flour

30 g (1 oz) cocoa powder

FOR THE CHOCOLATE GANACHE

700 g (1½ lb) plain, dark chocolate

300 ml (½ pint) buttermilk

TO ASSEMBLE

6 tbsp rum

45 g (1½ oz) chocolate, melted

8 Chocolate Fans (optional – see below)

1 Preheat oven to 180°C/350°F/Gas Mark 4. Grease and line a deep 20 cm (8 inch) loose-bottomed round cake tin.

2 Cream the butter with half of the sugar until light and fluffy. Gradually beat in the egg yolks.

3 Whisk the egg whites until they form stiff peaks. Gradually whisk in the remaining sugar to make a smooth, glossy meringue. Fold the meringue into the creamed mixture.

4 Sift the flour with the cocoa powder and fold into the mixture. Spoon into the cake tin and bake for 40 minutes or until firm to the touch. Leave in the tin for a few minutes, then turn out onto a wire rack; leave to cool completely.

5 To make the ganache, melt the chocolate in a bowl over a pan of simmering water. Bring the buttermilk almost to the boil. Remove from heat and stir in the melted chocolate. Allow to cool, then whip to a soft, spreading consistency.

6 Cut the cake into two layers and moisten with the rum. Sandwich together with half of the ganache. Smooth a third of the remaining ganache over the top and sides of the cake.

7 Place on a wire rack, set over a tray. Warm the remaining ganache to pouring consistency. Quickly pour on top of the cake and allow to spread down the sides. Vibrate the wire rack to get rid of air bubbles. Leave in a cool place to set.

8 Using a greaseproof piping bag, pipe zig-zag lines of melted chocolate on top of the gâteau. Position the chocolate fans around the side, if using, securing with a little melted chocolate.

CHOCOLATE FANS

1 Melt 100 g (3½ oz) chocolate in a bowl over a pan of simmering water, stirring until smooth. Let cool slightly until lukewarm.

2 Using a palette knife, spread the chocolate evenly on a warmed baking sheet, to a 24 cm (9½ inch) square. Leave in the refrigerator until set, then score into 8 x 3 cm (3½ x 1¼ inch) strips. With your index finger on the corner of a scraper blade, push the scraper at a 45° angle straight up each chocolate strip. The chocolate pushes together like a fan curling itself around your index finger.

Rich Chocolate Gâteau

STOLLEN

SERVES 8-10

120 ml (4 fl oz) milk
1 vanilla pod, split
15 g (½ oz) fresh yeast
300 g (10 oz) plain flour
pinch of salt
4 tbsp caster sugar
2 egg yolks
110 g (3¾ oz) unsalted butter
120 g (4 oz) raisins

60 g (2 oz) chopped mixed candied peel
finely grated zest and juice of 1 lemon
2 tbsp dark rum
35 g (1¼ oz) blanched almonds
60 g (2 oz) Marzipan (see page 34)

TO FINISH

unsalted butter, melted, for brushing
caster or icing sugar for dusting

1 Put the milk and vanilla pod in a pan and bring slowly to just below the boil. Cover and set aside to infuse for 20 minutes.

2 Discard the vanilla pod, then gently heat the milk, if necessary, until lukewarm. Pour into a small bowl, add the yeast and mix until creamy. Leave in a warm place for 10 minutes.

3 Sift the flour and salt into a large bowl. Stir in the sugar and make a well in the centre. Add the yeast mixture and egg yolks and gradually mix into the flour to form a dough. Knead for 5 minutes or until smooth. Cut the butter into pieces and scatter over the surface of the dough.

4 Cover the bowl with a damp cloth and set aside in a warm place to rise for 2-2½ hours or until doubled in bulk.

5 Meanwhile, combine the raisins, candied peel, lemon zest and juice, and rum in a bowl. Set aside to macerate. Spread the almonds on a baking sheet and toast under a preheated grill until golden; allow to cool.

6 Knead the risen dough gently, mixing in the butter completely. Add the drained fruit and toasted almonds and knead in until evenly distributed. Cover the bowl and refrigerate for at least 4 hours or overnight.

7 Turn the dough onto a lightly floured surface. Using a floured rolling pin, roll out to an oblong about 17.5 x 2.5 cm (7 x 5 inches), 2 cm (¾ inch) thick at one end, increasing to 4 cm (1½ inches) thickness at the other end, with a dip in the centre. Lift onto a baking sheet.

8 If using marzipan, shape into a log about 10 cm (4 inches) long and 2.5 cm (1 inch) in diameter; lay across the thicker end of the dough. Fold both ends of the dough over to meet in the centre, then fold the thick side over again. (The stollen should resemble a snail shell when viewed from the side.) Cover and leave to rise in a warm place for up to 3 hours.

9 Preheat oven to 200°C/400°F/Gas Mark 6. Bake the stollen for about 50 minutes until golden brown. Brush with melted butter and dust liberally with caster or icing sugar. Cool on a wire rack.

10 Wrap in greaseproof paper, then in foil. Store in an airtight container in a cool place and allow to mature for 2 weeks before serving.

INDEX